Praise for PassPorter®

PassPorter's Festivals and Celebrations book is another wonderful resource, especially for the repeat Walt Disney World guest. The attention to detail that is seen in all PassPorter books is here, of course. And for the person who is ready to move beyond a "regular" trip to the World, this is a wonderful elaboration on the many "extras" that Disney has to offer!

— Sandra Huling in Pennsylvania

Thank you for putting together this all inclusive guide to the various festivals and holiday celebrations at Walt Disney World. We are traveling to Walt Disney World soon and have the opportunity to attend Mickey's Very Merry Christmas Party during our stay. I was unsure whether the extra expense for the Christmas Party park ticket was worth it for my family. Your guide answered all my questions and we are joining the party!

— Patti Kalal in Illinois

I really love PassPorter's Festivals & Celebrations book because I learn all about what is going on each month so I can decide when I want to visit Walt Disney World.

— Laura Richardson in Colorado

Thank you for the Festivals and Celebrations book! It has helped me to get ready for my upcoming trip and take advantage of my Mickey's Very Merry Christmas Party ticket. I also learned how to get that extra special magic for my celebration. And thank you for reminding me not to expect the magic, but to just let it happen. Again thank you so much for the excellent books, e-books, and the forum.

— Lanita Wilkerson in Oregon

It's fun to read about the different parties, and to relive the fun and memories. Great photos!

— Beth Spellman in Massachusetts

I love how this book covers special events, from personal small ones to major holidays!

— Erin Rogers in Virginia

PassPorter's® Festivals and Celebrations at Walt Disney World®
by Thomas Cackler

© 2010 by PassPorter Travel Press, an imprint of MediaMarx, Inc.
P.O. Box 3880, Ann Arbor, Michigan 48106 • 877-929-3273
Visit us on the World Wide Web at http://www.passporter.com

PassPorter® is a registered trademark of MediaMarx, Inc.
Photographs © MediaMarx, Inc., unless otherwise noted

ISBN-13: 978-1-58771-095-7
ISBN-10: 1-58771-095-1

Version 1.2 (printed in October 2010)

PassPorter®'s
Festivals and Celebrations at Walt Disney World

Authored by Thomas Cackler
Edited by Carrie Hayward

PassPorter Travel Press

An imprint of MediaMarx, Inc.
P.O. Box 3880, Ann Arbor, MI 48106
877-WAYFARER
http://www.passporter.com

Party People

About the Author

"I'm going to Disney World!" That's what author **Thomas Cackler** said after returning to college and earning his bachelor's degree. Little did he know that this trip would kindle a new passion. Since 2002, Thomas has ventured to Walt Disney World three more times with his wife, Julie, and once with his nephew Joey. These trips, along with the constant planning and visits to popular Disney-related  message boards, have made Thomas a certified Disney nut! Thomas lives in Des Moines, Iowa, where he works as a web support technician and frequently asks anyone near a Disney park to say hi to Stitch for him. In addition to writing articles for PassPorter's weekly newsletter, Thomas has appeared on the Mouse Guest Weekly podcast to share his knowledge and love of all things Disney. As someone who looks for any excuse to party, Thomas hopes that this book will help bring a little extra magic to your next visit to Walt Disney World.

About the Editor

Carrie Hayward has edited newspaper, magazine, and web copy since 1994, but she's been a fan of Disneyland all her life. She and her husband, Patrick, try to visit the park monthly, and they especially enjoy date nights at Disneyland for swing dancing at Carnation Plaza Gardens. Carrie and Patrick also love Walt Disney World, where they were married in Epcot's Morocco Pavilion, and Tokyo DisneySea.

Acknowledgments

Thomas thanks his 'ohana for their encouragement during the writing of this book. You're the best! Carrie thanks her husband for sacrificing their "Muppet Show" nights so she could work on this book!

A special thanks to these very important folks "behind the scenes" at PassPorter Travel Press:

    Publishers: Jennifer and Dave Marx
    Layout and Design: Jennifer Marx
    Online Coordinator and Newsletter Editor: Sara Varney

Table of Contents

About This Book

PassPorter guidebooks are **independently published** by a family-owned and family-run small business. As journalists, we strive to present accurate information with a fair and balanced viewpoint. Our books are "unofficial," meaning we can call it as we see it.

We travel as our readers do. Although we enlist the help of local experts who live and breathe our destinations, we fly or drive long distances from our home bases, and stay in the hotels, giving us a perspective that no "local" can possess. We make all our own reservations and arrangements, sometimes with the help of a travel agent, but mostly we "shop direct." We pay our own way, so we're always looking for the best deal. We buy our own admission, pay for all our excursions, tours, and add-ons. We make our reservations through normal channels—no VIP treatment, no media discounts or freebies. We need to know that our experience will be like yours and hasn't been enhanced for the sake of a better review. While we may be invited to visit a hotel, restaurant, or attraction as members of the media, we do not use those visits to evaluate matters like quality of service or level of amenities offered, as regular guests may not receive quite the same treatment.

PassPorter guidebooks are truly a community effort. Through our PassPorter.com web site, message board community, PassPorter News weekly e-newsletter, and many face-to-face encounters, we interact with you, our readers, year-round. Whether or not we join a particular discussion, we're always watching the message boards to see what's important to you, and we're thinking of how we can better address those issues in our books. You contribute in so many ways! These pages are filled with your tips and photos, and your suggestions and questions over the years have led to improvements large and small. Your reports on our message board make you our field researchers, witnessing and experiencing far more than we could ever manage on our own. Dozens of you, as Peer Reviewers, pore over each manuscript, and each manages to uncover items to be updated, clarified, or fixed that nobody else has managed to find. Few publishers, in any field, subject their manuscripts to this level of scrutiny. Unlike many travel books, which, once printed, are set aside until it's time to produce the next edition, we're immersed in our topic 365 days a year, following the news and rumors, and keeping in constant touch with you.

All of this makes PassPorter a uniquely interactive guidebook. Together, we've created what we like to think of as "book 2.0" and we're proud to be innovators of a new generation of guidebooks that encourage collaboration. Here are some of the special interactive features in this edition:

PassPorter Photos: We truly believe that a picture tells a thousand words, and we include photos in the book whenever we can! The majority of these photos were contributed by our amazing readers, as we feel a wider range of perspective makes a better guidebook. All of the photos were hand-picked from our vast personal collection and the online PassPorter Photo Archive. The photos do not appear to their best advantage in black and white, as they are printed in this guidebook, however. We encourage you to go online to http://www.passporter.com/photos to view tens of thousands of photos in glorious color.

PassPorter Articles: You just can't fit everything in a guidebook, so when we have more to tell you, we lead you to a web address or article online. You'll find many more PassPorter articles at http://www.passporter.com/articles.

Chapter 1
Let's Party!

Every day is special to someone, and that alone is a reason to celebrate! The cast members at Walt Disney World know this quite well, and they roll out the red carpet for their guests daily. However, even Mickey and the gang like to celebrate extra-special events throughout the year. Whether it is an official festival that spans months or a quiet commemoration of a personal milestone, many revelers from around the globe choose to celebrate at Walt Disney World.

In addition to hosting holiday festivities and official events like Mickey's Very Merry Christmas Party, Walt Disney World partners with other organizations to host gatherings such as Atlanta Braves Spring Training and the Pop Warner Super Bowl. With festivals and celebrations that span both the calendar and the resort, there is something for everyone **every month of the year**. And the unique fireworks, parades, and entertainment that accompany seasonal events give even frequent visitors something new each time they come to Walt Disney World.

Yet all those options present a challenge to the average vacationer. Depending on the time of year, several extra events add to the already **overwhelming selection** of activities available at the Walt Disney World Resort. In December alone, more than a dozen special parties, festivals, and activities celebrate the holidays from just about every perspective. You may wonder, is this event included in my normal park admission? Will the parks be crowded? It can be quite a chore to work through this information and arrive at the resort prepared to have a good and relaxing time.

PassPorter's Festivals and Celebrations at Walt Disney World will help you choose the events that will make your upcoming vacation more magical or help you pick just the right time to visit the resort to participate in the party of your dreams. This book will break down events by type, ranging from exclusive, hard-ticketed parties to more casual celebrations. Each chapter includes information on what to expect (and what you might spend!) during each celebration, along with tips, tricks, and suggestions on how to maximize your experience.

Over the next few pages, we offer a calendar of events at Walt Disney World before diving in to **detailed descriptions of each celebration**. It is important to remember that while the calendar is a guideline, event dates and times are subject to change and will vary from year to year. Every effort is made to keep this book up-to-date, but for the very latest information, you should visit the PassPorter web site (http://www.passporter.com) along with the official Walt Disney World web site (http://disneyworld.com) for updates on times, dates, and prices.

Grab your silly hat and noisemaker—it's **time to party!**

Charting Your Course

Most vacation veterans will tell you that there is an ideal time to go to Walt Disney World. The same holds true if you want to experience the resort beyond the Tower of Terror and turkey legs. Just as some months are better for touring than others, **some months are better for experiencing seasonal events**. For example, many people will tell you that October is a great month to visit because of low crowds and cooler weather. However, October is also a great time to visit because of the Epcot International Food & Wine Festival and the multitude of Halloween happenings. This is perhaps the best feature of these events: Disney offers them during less-crowded times of the year to entice people to visit.

One important thing to remember is that while Disney is generally consistent with **event dates** from year to year, there are exceptions. For example, in 2007 *Star Wars* Weekends occurred entirely in the month of June, rather than in the traditional mid-May to mid-June time frame, due to a large *Star Wars* convention over Memorial Day Weekend that prevented appearances by the film's stars. While most of the major festivals are now annual occurrences, it is important to double check PassPorter's web site or the official Walt Disney World web site for the latest information (see links on page 7).

The following pages contain a **monthly list of seasonal events and festivals** at Walt Disney World. Each entry includes the event's home location and directs you to additional information within this book. When Disney makes a big deal out of a holiday, the calendar will note that as well. Feel free to skip around and compare events as you plan your perfect Walt Disney World celebration!

© Patrick Johnson

Mickey's Not-So-Scary Halloween Party runs from September through October

January
Walt Disney World Marathon Weekend (Resort-wide, page 45)

February
Atlanta Braves Spring Training (ESPN Wide World of Sports, page 40)
Champion 5K at ESPN the Weekend (Disney's Hollywood Studios, page 46)
Disney's Princess Half Marathon Weekend (Resort-wide, page 47)
President's Day Soccer Festival (ESPN Wide World of Sports, page 52)
Valentine's Day (Resort-wide, page 57)

March
Atlanta Braves Spring Training (Wide World of Sports, page 40)
Epcot International Flower & Garden Festival (Epcot, page 17)
Saint Patrick's Day (Resort-wide, page 62)

April
Disney Grad Nites (Disney's Hollywood Studios, page 33)
Easter (Resort-wide, page 58)
Epcot International Flower & Garden Festival (Epcot, page 17)

May
Cinco de Mayo (Resort-wide, page 62)
Columbia Muddy Buddy (page 48)
Danskin Orlando Triathalon (Resort-wide, page 50)
Disney Grad Nites (Disney's Hollywood Studios, page 33)
Epcot International Flower & Garden Festival (Epcot, page 17)
Florida Ironman 70.3 Triathlon (Fort Wilderness, page 49)
IronKids Orlando (Fort Wilderness, page 50)
Mother's Day (Resort-wide, page 58)

June
Disney's Pin Celebration (Epcot, page 37)
Father's Day (Resort-wide, page 59)
Gay Days (Unofficial event; resort-wide, page 35)
Sounds Like Summer Concert Series (Epcot, page 32)
Star Wars Weekends (Disney's Hollywood Studios, page 26)

July
Fourth of July (Resort-wide, page 59)
Sounds Like Summer Concert Series (Epcot, page 32)

September
Epcot International Food & Wine Festival (Epcot, page 12)
Expedition Everest Challenge (Animal Kingdom, page 47)
Mickey's Not-So-Scary Halloween Party (Magic Kingdom, page 21)
Night of Joy (Disney's Hollywood Studios, page 36)
Trek Women's Triathlon Series (Fort Wilderness, page 50)

Charting Your Course (continued)

October
Wine & Dine Half Marathon Weekend (Epcot, page 48)
Epcot International Food & Wine Festival (Epcot, page 12)
Halloween (Resort-wide, page 60)
Mickey's Halloween Family Fun Run 5K (Magic Kingdom, page 48)
Mickey's Not-So-Scary Halloween Party (Magic Kingdom, page 21)
Orlando International Dragon Boat Festival (Downtown Disney, page 50)

November
Candlelight Processional (Epcot, page 54)
Children's Miracle Network Classic (Palm & Magnolia Golf Courses, page 51)
Epcot International Food & Wine Festival (Epcot, page 12)
Festival of the Masters (Downtown Disney, page 38)
Mickey's Very Merry Christmas Party (Magic Kingdom, page 23)
Old Spice Classic (ESPN Wide World of Sports, page 52)
Osborne Family Spectacle of Dancing Lights (Disney's Hollywood Studios, page 55)
Thanksgiving (Resort-wide, page 60)

December
Candlelight Processional (Epcot, page 54)
Christmas, (Resort-wide, page 54)
Mickey's Jingle Jungle Parade (Animal Kingdom, page 55)
Mickey's Very Merry Christmas Parade (Magic Kingdom, page 54)
Mickey's Very Merry Christmas Party (Magic Kingdom, page 23)
New Year's Eve (Resort-wide, page 61)
Osborne Family Spectacle of Dancing Lights (Disney's Hollywood Studios, page 55)
Pop Warner Super Bowl and National Cheer and Dance Championships (ESPN Wide World of Sports, page 42)
Walt Disney World Christmas Day Parade (Magic Kingdom, page 54)

What Will You Celebrate?

Walt Disney World remains one of the best places to celebrate life's milestones. In fact, Disney encourages anyone celebrating anything from a first visit to a birthday to a wedding to note it on their hotel and dining reservations. There's also a portion of Disney's web site devoted to celebrations, at http://disneyworld.disney.go.com/celebrations/.

Check out Chapter 6 of this book for lots of great ideas about personal celebrations at Walt Disney World. If you're planning a wedding, honeymoon, or anniversary with The Mouse, see *PassPorter's Disney Weddings & Honeymoons* (http://www.passporter.com/weddings.asp/ for even more information.

Additionally, anyone who is celebrating should visit Guest Services at their resort hotel or at any of the theme parks to pick up a button announcing their special celebration. Whether it is a first visit, a birthday, an anniversary, or any other celebration, by wearing one of Disney's celebration buttons you'll be sure to get congratulations from cast members and fellow guests. And you may even get a few more surprises!

Chapter 2
Serious Partying
Multiweek & Ticketed Events

While Disney seldom misses an opportunity to market a holiday, certain festivals and celebrations **stand out above the rest**. These are major occurrences, and many fans plan their entire vacations around these events. Usually spanning multiple days, weekends, or even months, these events offer an extra opportunity for vacationers to experience the magic of Walt Disney World.

Ticketed events usually occur after park hours or in locations away from the general flow of traffic, and they can cost almost as much as a ticket to one of the parks. Tickets for many of these events go on sale in early May, with certain dates selling out early. Guests should visit http://www.disneyworld.com or call 407-WDW-PLAY for more information and to order tickets.

Festivals usually occur during park hours and are included with general park admission. Regardless of how Disney treats admission to these celebrations, each offers guests a wide variety of exciting entertainment opportunities.

While some guests plan their vacations around Walt Disney World's special events, most experience them as part of their **existing vacation plans**. Many of these festivals are designed as a way to increase traffic to the parks during off-peak travel times, when crowds are traditionally low. This allows savvy travelers to maximize their normal Walt Disney World vacation plans and still allow time to enjoy these festivals.

However, these festivals are also **incredibly popular with local residents**, especially those who already have annual passes to the parks. This means that vacationers who want to avoid the crowds will need to alter traditional touring plans if they are visiting during one of these special events. Proper planning is crucial to maximizing the fun and excitement of one (or more) of these festivals! Luckily, you've come to the right place.

The remainder of this chapter covers each **special event in more detail**. We've included costs, locations, and other important information to help you decide whether to visit Walt Disney World during one of these festivals. We also take a look at regular park attractions that will add to your festival experience. And our tips and tricks for each festival will help maximize the fun whether you plan your vacation around the experience or just hope to catch a little bit while enjoying the rest of your Walt Disney World vacation.

Epcot International
Food & Wine Festival

Held from late September through early November, the Epcot International Food & Wine Festival presents **world-class cuisine and wines** from the countries of the World Showcase and other regions, with special booths set up throughout the World Showcase area. While Epcot is always a showcase for fine dining from around the globe, the International Food & Wine Festival offers guests the opportunity to sample the cuisine in an expanded and less formal setting.

The fanciful festival sign near the front of Epcot

What Can I Expect?

The heart of this festival is the **International Marketplace**, food booths that dot the World Showcase. Each country represented has an area offering appetizer-sized portions of classic native dishes. While the offerings are not free, they are inexpensive, ranging from $2.25 to $7.00. These include classic dishes like sushi in Japan and crab cakes at the American Adventure, as well as wines, ales, beers, and other traditional beverages from each country.

In addition to the International Marketplace, the festival offers **seminars** on a wide range of culinary topics. Best of all, many of these events are free with park admission! These seminars, which range from 45 to 90 minutes long, run the gamut from cooking demonstrations to wine or beer tastings, with a little bit of everything in between. Epcot publishes a schedule for these seminars that can be found online prior to your arrival or in the park. Since seating is limited and the local residents are out in force, it is important to remember to arrive 30–45 minutes early for the event, especially if the topic is important to you.

Epcot also hosts the **Eat to the Beat concert series** during the International Food & Wine Festival. While today's biggest stars won't be found playing Epcot, the lineup offers classic artists like Little Richard and newer favorites like Big Bad Voodoo Daddy. With three shows nightly in the America Gardens Theater, chances are good that you'll catch at least one show if you are flexible with your time.

The International Food & Wine Festival offers a wide selection of **ticketed events**, known as "Festival Dining Experiences," including specialty wine and dinner pairings and the chance to dine with a celebrity chef. Is your appetite whetted yet? Good! Let's dive in to the main course and then sample a little of everything the festival has to offer.

International Marketplace

The heart and soul of the festival is the International Marketplace, **20 + food booths** offering national specialties from around the globe. Each World Showcase pavilion has its own booth representing at least one region from its country in addition to the regular food options. Several other countries have booths, from Argentina to

New Zealand and many points in between. As the host of both the festival and the World Showcase, the United States offers three pavilions.

Wellington, New Zealand booth

What sort of food will you find? Each booth presents **native specialties**, such as mofongo in Cuba and spanakopita in Greece. Most booths offer one or two savory options (usually an appetizer or side dish and a traditional main course) and a dessert.

Each year the International Food & Wine Festival features similar booths with slightly different menus. While you can expect some booths to offer the same thing every year, such as an escargot option in France or the famous Le Cellier Cheddar Cheese Soup in Canada, most **menus change** every time. You can visit http://allears.net/tp/ep/foodwine.htm to view current and past menus for reference. Here are a few photos with descriptions of some of the 2008 offerings.

Salmon with cheese soup in Canada

Churros and gazpacho in Spain

Apple strudel, spaetzle with mushroom ragout, and sausage in Germany

Lamb slider and scallops in New Zealand

© Patrick Johnson

The Festival Welcome Center is located inside the former Wonders of Life Pavilion

Festival Welcome Center

Located in the former Wonders of Life Pavilion, the Festival Welcome Center is the **launching point** for your International Food & Wine Festival experience. It is much more than just the festival gift shop—the pavilion also serves as the central location for many of the festival's special seminars and events. Official merchandise ranging from aprons to wine glasses is available for purchase. Also featured are the festival cookbook, which contains recipes for many of the foods you enjoy in the International Marketplace, and bottles of wine from each country. Just think of the Festival Welcome Center as a one-stop shop for enhancing your festival experience.

Eat to the Beat Concerts

The Eat to the Beat concerts usually occur at 5:15 pm, 6:30 pm, and 7:45 pm in the **America Gardens Theater**. The earlier shows tend to be more popular, and you should plan on arriving at least 30 minutes prior to show time if you want a seat near the front.

While you won't see new artists like the Jonas Brothers performing, you can catch several **classic artists** from decades gone by. The Beach Boys, Village People, Chubby Checker, and Boyz II Men have all performed during the festival. Be sure to check Steve Soares' Walt Disney World Entertainment web site for news on future concert performers: http://pages.prodigy.net/stevesoares/index.htm

---

⚈ The Disney Dining Plan and the Food & Wine Festival
Since the advent of the Disney Dining Plan, many people have asked if the tasting portions offered at the International Marketplace qualify as **snacks on the plan**. Most guests have reported that as long as the item is less than the current snack price limit ($4 as of this writing), the booth will accept a snack credit as payment. Be sure to check the menu posted at each booth, as these usually have items that qualify as a snack well marked.

Maximizing Regular Attractions

Epcot is known for embracing culture and technology. This means that there are already **several attractions and tours that fit in nicely** with the theme of the International Food & Wine Festival. The Land pavilion's Living With the Land takes guests on a boat ride through a greenhouse featuring fruits and vegetables grown using new and innovative technology. From the Mickey-shaped tomatoes to the unique soil-less method of growing crops, this tremendous attraction gives guests a behind-the-scenes look at where our food comes from.

Epcot also offers Behind the Seeds at Epcot, a **backstage tour** of The Land pavilion's greenhouses and fish farm. Guests get to sample vegetables grown on-site, feed the fish, and learn about innovative ways to maximize their personal gardens and landscapes back home! Tour cost is $16/adult ages 10 & up and $12/ages 3-9. Park admission to Epcot is also required. Sign up at the counter outside Soarin' (in The Land) or call 407-WDW-PLAY. Five tours are offered daily between 11:15 am and 4:30 pm.

Festival Dining Experiences

If you are a true food connoisseur, the Festival Dining Experiences are for you. Ranging from the multicultural Regional Feasts to up-close-and-personal Signature Dining with celebrity chefs, these events offer guests more palate-pleasing fun. While the Festival Dining Experiences are among the most expensive ticketed events that Walt Disney World offers, most guests would agree that they are worth the splurge.

First Bites Opening Reception
This kick-off event features samples from various Marketplace booths, wine seminars, demonstrations, and entertainment. If you want a chance to experience the Food and Wine Festival before everyone else, this event is for you!

Party for the Senses—Eat, Drink, and Celebrate
Guests start the evening with reserved seats at the Eat to the Beat concert series and then enjoy the handiwork of more than 25 chefs, accompanied by more than 70 wines and beers. Partygoers wander among the tasting stations and set props from Downtown Disney's Cirque du Soleil show, La Nouba.

"3D" Disney's Dessert Discovery
If you love dessert, then this party is for you. Held on select Thursday and Friday evenings during the festival, this 2½-hour event features a variety of sweet treats and cordials, plus access to a VIP viewing area for IllumiNations: Reflections of Earth.

Signature Dining
Are you hungry? Bring a big appetite as an all-star crew of celebrity and world-class Disney chefs team up to prepare a multicourse meal with wine pairings.

Regional Feasts
These special dinners takes guests on culinary trips to exotic regions around the globe, offering a four-course meal and performances by musicians from the featured countries.

Sweet Sundays
These are a great opportunity to satisfy a sweet tooth: Guests observe a celebrity pastry chef creating cakes, pies, and confections and get to sample the creations at a scrumptious continental breakfast.

The Cook, the Book, and the Bottle
Fans of celebrity chefs will watch the preparation of a delicious lunch and leave the meal with a commemorative bottle of wine and an autographed copy of one of the chefs' books.

Kitchen Conversations
Want to learn more about a celebrity chef? This seminar gives guests an opportunity to visit with a chef and learn how about his or her life in and out of the kitchen. After the seminar, guests receive an autographed copy of the chef's book.

Chefs A' Field - Kids on the Farm
Fans of the PBS television series *Chefs A' Field* will enjoy this special lunch with a featured chef. Guests enjoy a fantastic three-course lunch as they learn how produce and livestock make the journey from field to kitchen to plate. A complimentary copy of one of the *Chefs A' Field* books is included.

Epcot Wine Schools
If you'd like to learn about wines and what to look for in a great wine, this seminar will educate you and tempt your senses. Guests gain knowledge and a certificate of completion at the end of this all-day seminar.

Food & Wine Pairings
The restaurants of Epcot's World Showcase get into the act, offering tantalizing food and wine pairings at themed sessions moderated by a winemaker.

More Information

Disney rolls out new events each year, so be sure to check http://allears.net or http://www.foodwinefest.com/ for complete information.

Read Food & Wine Festival **guest experiences** in PassPorter trip reports at: http://www.passporterboards.com/forums/sharing-adventure-disney-world-trip-reports

---

Walt Disney World Swan and Dolphin Food & Wine Classic

This two-day event held in early October offers beverage seminars hosted by culinary experts from restaurants located at the Swan & Dolphin hotels, along with an evening reception featuring small bites from the various restaurants and live music. Cost for the event is $50/person for unlimited food and beverage samples, and advance purchase is required to attend the seminars. Alternatively, you may purchase individual tickets for a la carte sampling at a cost of $2/ticket or $45/25 tickets. The resorts offer special room packages that include party admission for each night's stay. Visit http://www.swandolphinfoodandwineclassic.com for more information.

Epcot International Flower & Garden Festival

Nothing makes Epcot come alive quite like the International Flower & Garden Festival. Held each spring (March 2-May 15 in 2011), this event brings the park into full bloom with special displays of terrific topiaries and all the color of spring. Many believe Epcot never looks as good as it does during the festival.

A beautiful topiary on display during the festival

In addition to the incredible horticultural displays, the festival showcases do-it-yourself experts who will help you turn your home into a similar work of art. Corporate sponsors provide **seminars** on successful home landscaping, and Epcot cast members give talks on the science behind the gardens and topiaries that decorate the park throughout the year.

Every night, the International Flower & Garden Festival brings the **Flower Power concert series** to the stage near the American Adventure pavilion. Favorite rockers from the '60s and '70s come back to celebrate memories of flower children and the Summer of Love. Best of all, these concerts are included in the cost of regular park admission. However, they do draw large crowds, so plan on arriving early for the best seats.

What Can I Expect?

The International Flower & Garden Festival is unique in that the point of the festival isn't massive amounts of activities for guests to experience. Instead, it focuses on a traditional approach to spring: **planting a new garden**. With its lush overlay of plantings and topiaries, Epcot truly looks its finest during the festival.

Each year brings a new theme. In 2011, Disney invites guests to "Celebrate the Great Outdoors." Past festival favorites include the Cinderellabration topiaries, the Pixie Hollow Playground, the interactive Pirates Adventure Zone, and topiaries of Belle and her Beast and that lovable rascal Stitch. While the events add to the fun, it's the topiaries that make Epcot truly come alive during the International Flower & Garden Festival.

Snow White and Dopey at the Germany pavilion

What Can I Expect? (continued)

Have you ever wondered how the pros keep the Disney parks looking so lush and green? During the festival, **Disney gardeners offer seminars** on turning your home garden or backyard into the same sculpted landscape that you see in the parks. These seminars are included with regular park admission, and they fill up fast, so plan on arriving up to an hour beforehand to ensure your entry.

Another fun festival activity is a visit to the Minnie's Magnificent Butterfly Garden. This distinctive **garden and butterfly house** contains hundreds of free-flying butterflies among the lush foliage. Additional activities can be found in the World Showcase, where each pavilion hosts a look at its gardening techniques. From the bonsai trees of Japan to the topiary trolls in Norway, these add an extra splash of color to the World Showcase and offer a deeper look into the way people in these countries live.

Theme Weekends

Each weekend during the International Flower & Garden Festival has a different theme, bringing with it **special guest speakers and extra activities**. Guests have the opportunity to view themed displays that reveal gardening tips and tricks from the masters, and most weekends feature character-hosted activities and fun for kids of all ages. In the past, these have included climbing at Pluto's Play Zone; Field Day activities like bean bag tosses and sack races; and the Kids Paint Out Experience, where budding artists are assisted by professional artists.

A topiary of feisty Stitch at the Flower & Garden Festival

Flower Power Concerts

Each night of the festival, the America Gardens Theater comes alive with the sounds of the **music of the '60s and '70s** as the Flower Power concert series takes center stage. You won't see Paul McCartney or Neil Young, but the lineup of talent is worth checking out. These concerts usually start at 5:15 pm, 6:30 pm, and 7:45 pm and are extremely popular with locals, so plan on arriving early for the best seats. Admission is free with park admission; no separate tickets are needed for the concerts.

While we can't guarantee certain artists will appear annually, bands such as Nelson, Gary Puckett, The Turtles, and Herman's Hermits have appeared in the past. Check **Steve Soares' Walt Disney World Entertainment web site** for news on concert performers: http://pages.prodigy.net/stevesoares/index.htm

Maximizing Regular Attractions

Among Epcot's permanent features is a tremendous attraction centered around gardening. Guests journey through the future of horticulture on The Land pavilion's **Living With the Land** ride. This attraction exposes guests to the cutting-edge technology and techniques being used in some magnificent gardens.

If you are looking for a behind-the-scenes experience, Epcot also offers Behind the Seeds at Epcot, a **backstage tour** of The Land pavilion's greenhouses and fish farm. In addition to learning how Epcot is developing new ways to landscape and garden, guests will sample vegetables grown on-site and get to feed the fish. Guests will also have the opportunity to learn about innovative ways to maximize their personal gardens and landscapes back at home! Cost is $16/ages 10 & up and $12/ages 3–9. You may make reservations up to 90 days in advance at 407-WDW-PLAY.

More Information

Visit **Disney's official web site** for the Flower & Garden Festival at: http://disneyworld.disney.go.com/parks/epcot/special-events/epcot-international-flower-and-garden-festival/

Look for the **free Festival Guide booklet**, available when you enter Epcot. The 24-page booklet details all the displays, tours, and events. It even includes handy maps!

Read a **PassPorter feature article** on the Flower & Garden Festival by Cheryl Pendry at http://www.passporter.com/articles/epcot-flower-garden-festival-disney.asp

Read Flower & Garden Festival **guest experiences** in PassPorter trip reports at: http://www.passporterboards.com/forums/sharing-adventure-disney-world-trip-reports

Magic Kingdom Seasonal Parties

Walt Disney World offers **two seasonal parties** at the Magic Kingdom. Winter brings Mickey's Very Merry Christmas Party, while fall features Mickey's Not-So-Scary Halloween Party. These ticketed parties occur after normal park hours and require an additional admission fee to attend. Each follows a similar format, offering special treats and exclusive entertainment, parades, and fireworks. Another perk is that select attractions are open and usually have short or no wait times. Best of all, the Magic Kingdom cast goes all-out to provide a magical experience sure to brighten your visit to the resort.

What's the Same?

The important thing to remember is that while each party has its own unique features and charm, the **basic concept and format are the same** for both seasonal parties. During the afternoon, day guests will start to see a transformation take place throughout the park. Special decorations will begin appearing throughout the Magic Kingdom during the late afternoon. The park will close approximately one hour prior to the party's official start time. While Disney doesn't widely promote this, they allow party guests entrance to the park as early as 4:00 pm when the party starts at 7:00 pm. This means party guests may enjoy some attractions before the event actually begins.

Once the party starts, the night is filled with special shows, fireworks, parades, and treats all **themed to the event**. Additionally, there are many opportunities to interact with various characters, including some who are harder to find during normal park hours. The party usually ends around midnight, so make sure you are well rested to maximize your enjoyment of the party.

Touring Tips

While the allure of walking right on to Splash Mountain may be strong, the key to enjoying these parties is to partake of the things you cannot do during a normal visit to the Magic Kingdom. If your schedule will allow it, you may want to visit the Magic Kingdom on **another day** to allow ample time to enjoy both the party and the park.

Parades and shows usually occur at least twice during a party, and the earlier they are, the more crowded they will be. If you and your group can handle it, plan on attending the **second or later of any show or event**. The crowds will be lighter, and you'll actually get more done during party hours because you won't spend as much time waiting for an event. Similarly, the later the hour gets, the smaller the crowds get. If you maximize your time at the party, you will find you can enjoy all the special events and be able to take that extra spin on Buzz Lightyear's Space Ranger Spin.

Mickey's Not-So-Scary Halloween Party

Fans of things that go bump in the night have a party just for them. Each September and October, Mickey Mouse hosts a Halloween party for all his friends at the **Magic Kingdom**, and the cast gets into the "spirit" of the holiday in grand style. With trick-or-treating, scary stories, haunted houses, costumes, a parade, and fireworks with one of the best soundtracks around, this family-friendly party offers something for everyone. Best of all, guests are encouraged to come in costume.

What's Different?

Scattered throughout the park are **trick-or-treat stations** sponsored by Goofy's Candy Company that allow guests to get their fill (and then some!) of sweet treats. The park is also filled with traditional Halloween frights. While Disney does try to keep the show family friendly, young children may find certain images and experiences too intense.

Mickey pumpkins are everywhere at Halloween!

The highlight of Mickey's Not-So-Scary Halloween Party is the **Happy HalloWishes fireworks spectacular**. With a soundtrack that highlights villains from all the classic Disney stories, along with a special trick-or-treat moment at Cinderella Castle, this fireworks show provides a truly memorable holiday experience. Mickey's Boo to You parade showcases many classic Disney characters in their holiday costumes.

Throughout the night, the **Disney Villains** take the stage in front of Cinderella Castle to show off their dastardliness. Afterward these evildoers take time to meet and greet guests, and there is no telling who might show up. Other character opportunities abound throughout the park, giving guests the chance to see less well-known characters along with their favorites, all in special holiday costumes.

In **Fantasyland**, guests can enjoy the Get Up and Boo-gie dance party. Fans of Experiment 626 will have the opportunity to dance with the little blue alien at Stitch's Dance Party in Tomorrowland. Also on hand is Merlin, who returns to the Magic Kingdom to show off his magic skills, along with live storytellers who haunt the streets of Liberty Square.

Cast members in party costumes

Mickey's Not-So-Scary Halloween Party (continued)

Maximizing Regular Attractions

There is one attraction that stands out as the most popular during the Halloween season, and it is often the most crowded. If you want to enjoy the **Haunted Mansion**, plan on doing so early in the evening to allow for more time to enjoy the special events. And for family-friendly thrills and chills, head to Snow White's Scary Adventure, Stitch's Great Escape, and Pirates of the Caribbean.

Party dates usually start in September and run through the weekend after Halloween. Ticket prices range from $57.46/adult and $51.07/child in advance to $63.85/adult and $57.46/child on the day of the event. Select dates offer a discounted rate of $53.20/adult and $46.81/child to Annual Pass holders and Disney Vacation Club members. Visit http://allears.net/tp/mk/mnssh.htm for the latest information and dates.

*Haunted Mansion
(lightning added for effect)*

Walt Disney World Railroad station decked out for the season

Mickey's Very Merry Christmas Party

The crown jewel of the Walt Disney World Resort holiday festivities, Mickey's Very Merry Christmas Party is a **picture-perfect holiday celebration**. If Disney's Hollywood Studios represent the Hollywood that never was yet always will be, then Mickey's Very Merry Christmas Party represents the holidays that never were but are what people dream they will be. Carolers, stories, cocoa, cookies, Santa, and Christmas trees all make this a party without equal.

What's Different?

The heart of this party is **Mickey's Very Merry Christmas Parade**. Shown twice nightly, it features not only characters in their holiday finest, but also marching wooden soldiers, magnificently decorated trees, and the first "snow" of the season on Main Street. While many of these elements are part of the annual television broadcast of the Walt Disney World Christmas Day Parade, seeing the parade at night is truly something special.

Between the parade showings is the special fireworks show, **Holiday Wishes**, featuring some of the most popular music of the season. But fireworks aren't the only special show of the night. In front of the castle, Celebrate the Season features classic Disney characters sharing gifts and holiday dreams with other holiday icons, like gingerbread men, snowmen, and classic toys. Just around the corner, Belle presents holiday tales in her Enchanted Garden.

Holiday decorations galore at the Magic Kingdom

Over in **Tomorrowland**, guests can dance the night away at the Cosmic Christmas Party or hear Mickey's rendition of "'Twas the Night Before Christmas" at the Galaxy Palace Theater. This retelling features many contemporary updates but remains true to the classic tale.

As at all special parties at the Magic Kingdom, **characters** are out and about, meeting, greeting, and signing autographs for guests. Of course the jolly old elf himself, Santa Claus, is on hand to meet guests just next to City Hall in Town Square. Fantasyland presents a bevy of characters and hosts the Holiday Hop dance party just outside of Ariel's Grotto.

Throughout the park, "**streetmosphere**" performers, singers, and improv acts provide continuous entertainment, and guests are invited to enjoy hot cocoa, cookies, apple slices, and cider all evening.

Mickey's Very Merry Christmas Party (continued)

Maximizing Regular Attractions

Because the Magic Kingdom's regular lineup of attractions come about as close to Christmas as Dad does to not burning the holiday meal in the last scene in the Carousel of Progress, most attractions have **low wait times** during Mickey's Very Merry Christmas Party. While it is still a good idea to visit the Magic Kingdom another day to enjoy all the regular attractions, most partygoers report that it is easy to enjoy regular attractions during the party, even later in the evening.

The dates for Mickey's Very Merry Christmas Party usually **begin in mid-November** and run through the week before Christmas. Ticket prices range from $57.46/adult and $51.07/child in advance to $63.85/adult and $57.46/child on the day of the event. Select dates offer a discounted rate of $53.20/adult and $46.81/child to Annual Pass holders and Disney Vacation Club members. Please visit http://allears.net/tp/hol_mk.htm for this year's dates as they are announced.

> **Party Videos**
> Want to see more of what these seasonal Magic Kingdom parties have to offer? Many fans have posted their **home videos** of these events online. Watching their footage of the parades, the fireworks, and all the festivities in between, you get a good feel for what to expect. Search for the party you're interested in at a video web site like YouTube (http://www.youtube.com).

© 2007 Denise Preskitt (http://www.mousesteps.com)

Cinderella Castle covered in "Dream Lights" like a glistening blanket of ice

Chapter 3
Weekend & Multiday Events

Not every celebration at Walt Disney World is a multiweek festival or ticketed event. The resort offers numerous **shorter events** that yield as much fun and entertainment as their big brothers. These weekend celebrations give guests the chance to live out such dreams as becoming a soap star, training as a Jedi Knight, or competing with professional athletes, all at the place where dreams come true. Best of all, most of these events occur during regular park hours and are included in the cost of park admission!

As with the bigger festivals, Disney uses these weekend events to promote other brands within the company (like ESPN), celebrate special milestones (Grad Nites), and draw guests into the park (*Star Wars* Weekends). Disney is working hard to **eliminate the off-season** at the resort, and it just might be working—these events draw a different crowd to the parks than the larger festivals do, which means more customers for Disney.

This chapter also includes information on one of the biggest unofficial festivals on property: **Gay Days**. This is a community-driven celebration, and Disney does not recognize it in any way. However, the event does have an impact on the resort, and guests who are visiting during this time should plan accordingly.

We've divided this chapter into sections covering each of these special events in more detail. Our **travel tips and touring suggestions** will allow you to determine whether an event is for you or if you should avoid a particular park during your trip. Each section will also include a brief description of the impact these special events have on the entire resort.

So grab your party hats and autograph pen—**there's more to partying** at Walt Disney World than you might realize!

Star Wars Weekends

If you long for lightsabers as much as you love Mickey Mouse, Disney has just the event for you. Each year in late spring, **Disney's Hollywood Studios** come alive with the sights, sounds, and fun of the *Star Wars* universe during Walt Disney World's *Star Wars* Weekends. With Star Tours as the event's home base, the park becomes the place for Jedi and Sith alike to enter that galaxy far, far away and enjoy the magic that only director George Lucas and Disney can provide.

What Can I Expect?

The heart and soul of the *Star Wars* Weekends experience are the characters and the actors who brought them to life, and they are everywhere. The interaction between guests and characters is the **event's main draw**, from the gauntlet of Storm Troopers at the front gates to the opportunity to ask actor Peter Mayhew just how hot it was inside his Chewbacca costume. The key thing to remember is that since the events are free with paid park admission, they tend to fill quickly. Guests are encouraged to arrive early for both their park day and the events they wish to attend.

Each weekend, 30–40 **costumed characters** from the *Star Wars* movies appear for photos and autographs. In the past, these have included Luke Skywalker, Princess Leia, R2-D2, Chewbacca, Ewoks, Mace Windu, Shaak Ti, Kit Fisto, Anakin Skywalker, Queen Amidala, Jedi Mickey, Darth Sidious, Darth Maul, Jawas, Clone Troopers, the Cantina Band, Darth Vader, Storm Troopers, Sand Troopers, Tusken Raiders, Gamorrean Guards, and Greedo.

As if meeting a Dark Lord of the Sith isn't enough, *Star Wars* Weekends also gather **actors** from the entire *Star Wars* saga. While you probably won't meet Hayden Christensen or Harrison Ford, the actors who do come really appreciate the fans and take time for pictures and autographs. Previous guests have included Warwick Davis (Wicket the Ewok), Bonnie Piesse (Beru Lars), Kenny Baker (R2-D2), Ray Park (Darth Maul), Daniel Logan (young Boba Fett), Jeremy Bulloch (Boba Fett), Peter Mayhew (Chewbacca), Anthony Daniels (C-3PO), and Amy Allen (Aayla Secura), to name a few.

Darth Vader appears onstage near Star Tours

Many of the same actors appear in the daily "**Stars of the Saga**" talk show and Q&A session hosted by Jay Laga'aia (Captain Typho). This is a great opportunity for fans to ask questions about the actors' experiences filming the *Star Wars* saga. Each day of the event also features an additional parade, Legends of the Force: A *Star Wars* Celebrity Motorcade. With the entire Florida garrison of the *Star Wars* fan community of Storm Troopers, known as the 501st Legion, marching along, this is a very impressive parade.

Young Padawans can exhibit their prowess with the Force as they learn to become a **Jedi in the Jedi Training Academy**. Held throughout the day, the show gives young guests the opportunity to train with a Jedi and learn a few lightsaber moves. Midway through the training, however, Darth Vader and Darth Maul interrupt and try to harm the Padawan and the Jedi Master (see photo). Hopefully the young Jedi has learned enough to defeat the Dark Lord of the Sith. This interactive show is so popular that it has become part of the daily entertainment at Disney's Hollywood Studios and at Disneyland in California.

Darth Maul parries with a Padawan and a Jedi Master during Jedi Training Camp

But *Star Wars* Weekends aren't just about the character interaction. Jedi Padawans can show off their *Star Wars* knowledge with the **Padawan Mind Challenge**, the *Behind the Force* film gives fans a sneak peek into the creative mind of *Star Wars* creator George Lucas, and the Hyperspace Hoopla ends each day's festivities by combining the two most popular things in 1977 (disco and *Star Wars*) in a party outside of Star Tours. If you thought Chewbacca was impressive in the movies, just wait until you see him imitate John Travolta from *Saturday Night Fever*.

Jabba's Hutt

If there are two things that Disney fans and *Star Wars* fans share, it's that they love their characters and they **love to collect**. It should come as no surprise that the event offers a wide selection of exclusive merchandise, which is so popular that the Tatooine Traders shop at the exit of Star Tours can't hold it all.

Collectors and fans have the **opportunity to purchase** *Star Wars* pins, exclusive plush toys, T-shirts, hats, and more. Most popular are the "big fig" (large scale) sculptures of Disney characters costumed as *Star Wars* characters. In 2009, the last series of the popular Disney big figs hit the market, with Mickey as Luke Skywalker training with Yoda on his back, Goofy as Chewbacca, Donald Duck as Han Solo encased in carbonite, and Minnie Mouse in the infamous Princess Leia slave costume from *Return of the Jedi*.

Maximizing My Experience

Of course the most popular attraction during *Star Wars* Weekends is **Star Tours**. Since the ride serves as a hub of activity for the event, waits can be long.

Fans of George Lucas' films will also enjoy the Indiana Jones Epic Stunt Spectacular!, while the Studios Backlot Tour has some Star Wars vehicles in the "boneyard" section.

The important thing to remember is that visiting the park for this event means **less focus on the park attractions** and more on the special activities. If *Star Wars* is not your cup of tea, you may be tempted to skip Disney's Hollywood Studios on the *Star Wars* Weekends dates. However, most of the events (and crowds) will be on the Star Tours side of the park, which means that popular attractions like The Twilight Zone Tower of Terror and Rock 'n' Roller Coaster starring Aerosmith won't be as busy as you'd expect.

Dave Marx practices his saber skills on the AT-AT Walker

Dates & Guests

Star Wars Weekends begin in either **late May or early June** and run for four consecutive weekends. The event ran for six weekends in years past, but in 2007 it was scaled back to the current four weekends. The event has run annually since 2000, only skipping 2002—the year of *Star Wars* Celebration II. Disney usually announces the dates in December or January. In 2010, *Star Wars* Weekends were held May 21-23, May 28-30, June 4-6, and June 11-13.

For more information, check http://allears.net/tp/mgm/m_starwars.htm or http://www.studiocentral.com

Previous guests have included Warwick Davis, Kenny Baker, Ray Park, Daniel Logan, Peter Mayhew, Jeremy Bulloch, Anthony Daniels, David Prowse, and Bonnie Piesse. Be sure to visit http://www.starwars.com/fans/news/ or http://allears.net/tp/mgm/m_starwars.htm for a complete guest list each year.

Star Tours: The Adventures Continue

In 2011, Star Tours will reopen from a lengthy refurbishment just in time for *Star Wars* Weekends. The improvements will include multiple randomly determined adventures to new destinations, high-definition video, a Disney Real-D 3D screen, an improved motion simulator, and several new special effects. Visit http://passporter.com or http://www.starwars.com for more information on the new attraction once it becomes available.

ESPN The Weekend

What do Stuart Scott and Donald Duck have in common? Aside from working for Mickey Mouse, they'll both be hanging out at Disney's Hollywood Studios during ESPN The Weekend. This three-day event brings all the excitement of the sports network to Walt Disney World. Not only do the **celebrities of ESPN** broadcast live from the park, they bring along famous athletes from across the sports spectrum. Best of all, this event, which is usually held in late February or early March, is free with regular park admission.

What Can I Expect?

ESPN The Weekend gives Disney an opportunity to cross-promote two of their **most popular properties**: theme parks and the "Worldwide Leader in Sports." The event offers a wide variety of hands-on sports activities, interaction with athletes and celebrities, and even an opportunity to showcase your skills as a *SportsCenter* anchor.

The heart and soul of ESPN The Weekend are the **live broadcasts** that originate from underneath Mickey's Sorcerer Hat just outside of The Great Movie Ride. Unlike some of Disney's other special events, this one offers significant A-list talent. ESPN television shows like *SportsCenter*, *NFL Live*, *Baseball Tonight*, and *Cold Pizza* broadcast live as part of the celebration. ESPN Radio shows like *Mike & Mike in the Morning* and *The Herd With Colin Cowherd* also broadcast live from the park. Chances are good you'll see some of your favorite on-air talent at the park.

Near Rock 'n' Roller Coaster Starring Aerosmith is the **ESPN Sports Zone**, an interactive area where guests can try out professional sports like football, hockey, racing, and basketball. Designed for the whole family, the ESPN Sports Zone also offers guests an opportunity to see what it's like to sit behind the *SportsCenter* desk. Whether you're making or reporting the sports news, you'll get to let the world know who has the right stuff.

ESPN The Weekend (continued)

Many of the featured athletes participate in a **daily motorcade** through the streets of Disney's Hollywood Studios, giving you an even better chance of seeing your favorites. Guests also have a chance to ask questions and get to know the stars better in the daily conversations on the main stage and at the Post Game Interview sessions. Plus, guests can go backstage and hear the inside scoop firsthand from the on-air talent at the Inside ESPN seminars.

PassPorter fan Christy Henise-Kohr goes one-on-one with a member of the Harlem Globetrotters

For the sports expert, ESPN The Weekend offers a chance to play a live version of the popular ESPN game show **Stump the Schwab**. This all-star version gives guests the opportunity to showcase their sports-trivia knowledge in teams of three along with a sports celebrity. Fans on the winning team will proceed to a final-round showdown with Howie Schwab himself!

Fans of ESPN's reality show Dream Job, where contestants compete for a real SportsCenter job, can participate in a **live version of the show** where the audience selects the winner. Get your camera ready, because celebrities drop by during the competition to offer some helpful tips!

Disney also offers the Champion 5K at ESPN The Weekend race, which sends runners through Disney's Hollywood Studios and benefits the V Foundation for Cancer Research. More information on the race can be found on page 46.

Tip: If you can't make it to ESPN The Weekend, tune in to ESPN on your TV on the weekend of the event—you'll see Walt Disney World and glimpses of various events as ESPN reports live!

More Photos of Festivals and Celebrations

The PassPorter Photo Archive at http://www.passporter.com/photos has hundreds of photos of the various festivals, celebrations, and holidays at Walt Disney World. Search on the specific event name or just type in "festival" as your search word.

Maximizing My Experience

Sports fans have a wide variety of activities to enjoy at ESPN The Weekend. Disney's Wide World of Sports Complex hosts the **Atlanta Braves' spring training** (see page 40), and there's usually at least one game during the event. Even if you can't make it to a game, you may be able to check out a practice or two. Visit http://www.disneysports.com/atlantabraves for more information.

Baseball isn't the only sport offered on the property. **Golf fans** can partake of several championship golf courses, including Disney's Magnolia and Palm courses, which host the Children's Miracle Network Classic each November (see page 51). If you prefer to struggle with windmills rather than with water hazards, the resort also boasts two of the best miniature golf courses in the country: Fantasia Gardens and Disney's Winter Summerland.

Guest List

While the guest list for ESPN The Weekend changes each year, the caliber of celebrities is usually the same. Since Disney views this as a cross-promotional opportunity, they bring out ESPN's biggest names, including past participants Colin Cowherd, Mike Golic, Peter Gammons, and the aforementioned Stuart Scott. Such athletes as Tony Dorsett, Bret Favre, and Kurt Warner from the NFL; Curt Schilling, CC Sabathia, and Derek Lowe from MLB; Scottie Pippen from the NBA; and Olympic great Shawn Johnson headline the list. For the current list of celebrities, as well as highlights from previous events, visit http://www.espntheweekend.com.

More Information

The official ESPN The Weekend site is at http://www.espntheweekend.com.

Special events like ESPN The Weekend draw crowds to Disney's Hollywood Studios

Sounds Like Summer Concert Series

Is that Garth Brooks? Did ABBA reunite for one last show? Not likely, especially if it is summer and the concert is at the America Gardens Theater in Epcot. Each summer, the sounds of some of the most popular recording artists come not from the acts themselves but from the ultimate lineup of **tribute bands**, who cover all the hits at Disney's Sounds Like Summer Concert Series.

What Can I Expect?

Each night one tribute act takes the stage three times at the **America Gardens Theater**. While these performers may not be dead ringers for the musicians they emulate, their performances are truly tributes to some of the best acts in contemporary music.

Shows are spaced approximately **one hour apart**, at 5:45 pm, 7:00 pm, and 8:15 pm. As with all free shows at Walt Disney World, the theater may fill up quickly, so plan accordingly. Earlier shows may be especially crowded because they are around popular dining times.

Maximizing My Experience

One of the best parts of Epcot is the **acts who regularly perform** throughout the World Showcase. Enjoying performances by Beatles tribute band The British Invasion, MoRockin', and Off Kilter earlier in the day would extend the music theme of your Epcot experience.

Another great musical experience at Epcot is the classical soundtrack of the film *Impressions de France*. Also, many pavilions around the World Showcase feature music, such as the drummers in Japan or strolling mariachi bands in Mexico. Whether your taste is classical or contemporary, Epcot offers you a world of musical possibilities.

Concert Lineup

Past performers include Slippery When Wet (Bon Jovi), Bjorn Again (ABBA), Hotel California (Eagles), Transit Authority (Chicago), and Captain Fantastic (Elton John). Visit Steve Soares' Walt Disney World Entertainment web site for news on future concert performers: http://pages.prodigy.net/stevesoares/index.htm.

Disney Grad Nites

High school seniors can celebrate the milestone of graduation at all-night parties known as Disney Grad Nites. Although these have been held at Disney's Hollywood Studios in years past, 2010 marked the event's return to the **Magic Kingdom**. Hot music, good friends, and some of Disney's most intense attractions combine for one incredible evening of Disney magic.

What Can I Expect?

Disney Grad Nite is a series of **private parties for high school seniors** and their chaperones. While Disney offers these ticketed events on various dates, they usually happen on Friday and Saturday nights in late April and early May. Disney Grad Nite now starts at 8 pm and lasts until 2 am. The cost is $53.80/person. Disney requires one chaperon for every 10 grads attending, but one complimentary chaperon ticket is offered for every 10 grads.

In addition to keeping attractions open throughout Grad Nites, Disney brings in **popular music acts** to entertain throughout the evening. The traditional background music in the parks gives way to contemporary music and tunes spun by a DJ.

Disney takes **security and safety** at these events seriously. All guests must adhere to a dress code (see the chart on the next page) and undergo a security screening prior to entering the park. Inside, Disney steps up security, deploying high-profile security officers to join regular cast members and the chaperones. Disney considers this a school event and insists that chaperones enforce all school policies in addition to Disney's party rules.

Maximizing My Experience

As you might expect, the kids at Disney Grad Nites are all about one thing: **thrills**! With the event back at the Magic Kingdom, lines are usually longest for the mountains and the "cool" rides, leaving classics like The Many Adventures of Winnie the Pooh and "it's a small world" with short or no lines.

Since Disney Grad Nites are limited to graduating seniors, other visitors should **note the dates of these parties** and remember that the Magic Kingdom will close earlier on these days. Many groups make this their senior trip, visiting the resort for the entire weekend, and the Value resorts usually will get the majority of these visitors.

Dress Code Guidelines

It's dress to impress time! Check the online dress code guidelines for changes at:
http://disneyyouthgroups.disney.go.com/program/show/12?subdid=3

Acceptable for Guys	Acceptable for Girls
Casual pants (including khakis, shorts, and jeans), shirts with collar (golf-style shirts, dress shirts), sport jackets, dress suits, comfortable shoes (including tennis shoes, sandals, dress shoes, and boots).	Dresses, skirts, shorts, casual pants (including jeans), blouses, and tops, and comfortable shoes (including tennis shoes, dress sandals, and boots).

Unacceptable for All

- Any clothing affiliated with a school, professional sports team, group, club, etc. (Chaperones and faculty members will be permitted to wear school-affiliated golf shirts or polos.)
- Clothing not in good repair (torn jeans, pants, shirts, etc.). Jeans are okay as long as they are not ripped or torn.
- Revealing clothing (i.e., bathing suit tops or bottoms, cropped tops, see-through clothing, etc.).
- Hats and/or bandanas (either worn or hanging from belt loops, pockets, etc.).
- Chains or spiked accessories; oversized belts and necklaces.
- All backpacks. Small purses and hip bags are okay.
- Weapons, knives, laser pointers, or chemical irritants are not permitted. Students or chaperones not following this guideline will be dealt with at the discretion of the Orange County Sheriff's Office.
- Alcohol and tobacco products are not allowed and will be confiscated and not returned if found on-site.

8th Grade Grad Jam!
Just entering high school rather than leaving it? Don't worry, Walt Disney World has you covered! Disney hosts the 8th Grade Grad Jam for youth graduating from middle school. The biggest difference with this party is the hours (7:30 pm to 11:30 pm). Otherwise, kids enjoy many of the same types of events their older friends do at Grad Nite, including a DJ dance party, dinner, and lots of Disney magic. Visit http://disneyyouthgroups.disney.go.com/program/show/16?subdid=11 for more information.

Gay Days

Gay Days, held annually in **late May or early June,** draws more than 150,000 gay and lesbian Disney fans from around the country to Orlando for a unique and very unofficial festival. Many of the events are held off Disney property, but each park has a designated day for participants to visit and show their spirit by wearing red shirts (see photo below). Get details at http://www.gaydays.com.

Guests who want to **avoid the crowds** should check the Gay Days schedule if they have a trip planned during this time (because this is an unofficial event, these park days are not listed on Disney's event calendars).

A view of Main Street, U.S.A. during Gay Days

Night of Joy

Fans of **contemporary Christian music** and Walt Disney World, rejoice! Disney offers a weekend of incredible music and theme-park fun just for you. Held annually in September, Night of Joy features in-park concerts by some of the genre's most popular artists, and select rides and attractions remain open for concertgoers to enjoy. Held at the Magic Kingdom, Night of Joy has been combining the hope of contemporary Christian music and the wonder of Disney for three decades.

What Can I Expect?

With its combination of entertainment and access to regular attractions, Night of Joy is similar to the ticketed after-hours events at the Magic Kingdom. Four **different stages showcase the various acts simultaneously**, so it is important to remember that you probably won't see every act. However, Disney does a good job of making sure that the headlining artists aren't playing at the same time.

Following a similar pattern to other ticketed events, Night of Joy offers guests the opportunity to **enjoy favorite attractions** in addition to rocking the night away.

It is important to note that Night of Joy is **popular with youth groups**. In fact, Disney aggressively markets this event to churches throughout the South. As a result, the majority of attendees are teenagers with varying levels of supervision. While most are respectful and well behaved, they are still teenagers, so plan your visit accordingly.

© Brenda Pede

Night of Joy 2003

Maximizing My Experience

As with all ticketed events at Disney, guests may want to allow another day to tour Disney's Hollywood Studios and **set aside the concert times** for watching the acts. Since Night of Joy occurs on a Friday and Saturday, the Studios will most likely be busier than normal that weekend as concertgoers fill the park prior to the show.

Concert Schedule

With one of the widest ranges of performers assembled in one place, Night of Joy offers something for every musical taste. Previous performers have included MercyMe, Skillet, Jars of Clay, Michael W. Smith, Newsboys, Chris Tomlin, and Superchick. To find the latest information on the lineup, visit http://www.nightofjoy.com.

Event Costs

In 2010, one-night tickets cost $49.95/person in advance and $57.95 on the day of the event. Two-night tickets cost $89.95/person in advance. Discounts are available for groups of 10 or more by calling 877-NITE-JOY or visiting http://www.nightofjoy.com.

More Information

Visit the official web site for the Night of Joy at http://www.nightofjoy.com.

Disney's Pin Celebration

If you are a fan of the popular collectible Disney pins, there's an event just for you! Epcot hosts Disney's Pin Celebration, a special event for die-hard collectors, each year in mid- to late-September. Special trading opportunities, games, and activities give pin fans an opportunity to expand their collections, and unique pins created specifically for this event are a big draw. Disney's Pin Celebration occurs during normal park hours but requires separate admission of $115. Each participant receives $30 in food and beverage gift cards and has the opportunity to purchase limited-edition pins, attend auctions for preproduction pins, meet Disney Pin Partners, and purchase other limited-edition gifts. Pin trading fans should visit http://eventservices.disney.go.com/pintrading/index for more information.

Festival of the Masters

For more than 30 years, one weekend in November has brought to Downtown Disney's West Side an **incredible display of art** as part of the Festival of the Masters. More than 150 award-winning artists from around the country display their original creations in this one-of-a-kind art show and competition, and judges select the best entries in sculpture, jewelry, painting, photography, glass, and digital art categories.

But it's not just about looking at the art—this festival offers something for the **entire family**. In addition to the main art show, the festival has featured more than 6,000 square feet of sidewalk decorated by the Central Florida Chalk Artists Association, along with the "Where the Art Meets the Soul" Folk Art Festival at the House of Blues. The festival also offered kids a chance to unleash their inner artists at interactive art zones, including a kids' sidewalk-painting area. Additionally, Disney performance artists Trevor Carlton and Stephen Reis created an original masterpiece outside the Virgin Megastore that was then available at auction. Best of all, the entire festival is free to visit.

Festival of the Masters is typically held during the **second weekend in November**. Each day usually runs from 9:30 am to 5:30 pm, with an awards ceremony on the afternoon of the last day, usually at 3:00 pm. Festival of the Masters typically coincides with Veterans Day, which means higher crowds and less availability at the resorts. The festival may also coincide with what is known as "Jersey Week," a period when school is out in New Jersey schools for teacher conferences and Walt Disney World sees an influx of vacationers from the Garden State.

More Information

Guests looking for **more information** about Festival of the Masters should visit http://www.disneyworld.com/artfestival.

You can view many **photos** of the Festival of the Masters at a fellow vacationer's gallery at http://www.pbase.com/mschiff/festivalofthemasters2006.

Chapter 4
Special Sporting Events

Walt Disney World offers a **wide variety** of sporting events and competitions, ranging from holiday tournaments featuring amateurs to excellent professional sporting events and training. Nearly every month offers something different for sports fans. Since we've already looked at ESPN The Weekend (see page 29), this chapter will focus on the multitude of spectator and participatory sports Walt Disney World has to offer.

If you are a runner, Disney offers **multiple opportunities** to participate in races, ranging from 5K runs to the popular full marathon. If watching sports is more your speed, you can enjoy everything from professional baseball, football, and golf to amateur basketball or football. Chances are good that if you are a fan of a particular sport, Walt Disney World has an event for you.

As they say in real estate, location is everything. This is also true with sporting events at Walt Disney World. Since most of the Disney parks lack the necessary space and venues to host these events (alas, there is not a place big enough for a baseball diamond at any of the parks), the focus shifts to the **ESPN Wide World of Sports Complex**. This state-of-the-art facility hosts the majority of these events and gives the average guest a reason to venture beyond the parks.

This chapter breaks the events into categories and then takes a **closer look** at each event. While Disney often publishes schedules months ahead of time, some events aren't promoted until just before they occur. As always, for the latest information, head over to http://www.passporter.com or Walt Disney World's official site for the ESPN Wide World of Sports Complex, at http://espnwwos.disney.go.com/complex/. The official site offers up-to-the-minute information on upcoming events, including ticket-purchasing information.

Now it's time to **lace up your sneakers** and get ready to cheer. Tons of sporting fun awaits!

Atlanta Braves Spring Training

The Atlanta Braves hold spring training at Champion Stadium (formerly The Ballpark/ Cracker Jack Stadium) at the ESPN Wide World of Sports Complex. This may not be the players' favorite time of the year, but it does give the average fan an opportunity to watch favorite players hone their craft in pursuit of a world championship.

What Can I Expect?

Training camps are a time for players, coaches, and other team personnel to get back into the swing of things after the off-season. For the Braves, this means spending part of February and most of March playing real games against other Grapefruit League teams. (The Grapefruit League consists of all the Major League Baseball teams who train in Florida.) For the fans, these months provide a great opportunity to see how a professional team prepares for contests and give them a chance to score an elusive autograph.

Spring training is like an extension of the regular season. Daily games are common, although not every game features every player. In 2011, the Braves' schedule includes 16 spring training games at Champion Stadium, which is consistent with previous years' schedules. Dates are listed on the Braves' official web site (http://www.atlantabraves.com). Depending on your seat, the cost of these games ranges from $15-$32. As with regular season games, fans who arrive early can watch batting practice and have an opportunity to get autographs.

Visit http://www.atlantabraves.com or http://www.ticketmaster.com for more information.

Disney added new features for spring training games in 2009, including a unique on-field spectator experience where fans can watch batting practice and pre-game warm-ups from behind home plate. The cost is $75/person and includes a disposable camera. Additionally, Disney offers fans an all-you-can-eat buffet of ballpark food for $18.95/person. There are also plans for several themed nights and lots of interaction with the classic Disney characters. Visit http://espnwwos. disney.go.com/events/pro/braves-spring-training/or http://www.ticketmaster. com. Those traveling from outside the Orlando area can visit http://www. springtrainingtours.com for special travel packages.

Maximizing My Experience

Fans should **make plans early** to attend practices and games. It is also important to remember that these are for team evaluation, and many times the bigger stars may not practice or play. However, these events are often a great chance to get a look at the stars of tomorrow and to see the sports up close and in person.

Since buses don't run as often to the ESPN Wide World of Sports Complex, fans should **allow ample travel time** to a practice or game. The only bus transportation available to the complex leaves from Disney's Hollywood Studios. You may want to consider driving yourself or calling a taxi to ensure you arrive on time. If you drive, follow the signs to Osceola Parkway East/ESPN Wide World of Sports and turn south onto Victory Way. In addition, dining options are limited to the food court, which replaced the complex's table-service restaurant, so you may want to make alternative plans.

More Information

Get a **detailed map** and information on the free wi-fi zones at the ESPN Wide World of Sports Complex at http://espnwwos.disney.go.com/.

You can **get recorded information** by calling 407-939-FANS or speak to a guest services representative by calling 407-939-1500.

Champion Stadium at the ESPN Wide World of Sports Complex

Pop Warner Super Bowl and National Cheer and Dance Championships

Each year thousands of youngsters take the field to participate in organized Pop Warner leagues, a national network of youth football and cheerleading programs. These pint-sized football players share a dream with their counterparts in the National Football League: to win the Super Bowl. Although the location of the NFL Championship changes every year, the Pop Warner Super Bowl stays put at the **ESPN Wide World of Sports Complex**. Also held during this time are the National Cheer and Dance Championships for organized cheerleading teams. Every year, early December brings football teams, spirit squads, and families from across North America to Walt Disney World to determine who is the best of the best.

What Can I Expect?

The Pop Warner Super Bowl and National Cheer and Dance Championships bring many young fans and families to Walt Disney World. As a result, the Value resorts, especially All-Star Sports, tend to **attract a heavy concentration of youngsters** and their families. Most of the activities are held at the ESPN Wide World of Sports Complex, but teams that are not competing or training often head out to enjoy the parks.

If you plan to participate in the Super Bowl as a player, coach, or spectator, here's how it works: The categories of competition are broken down into traditional Pop Warner weight and age classifications. Each team that advances to the national competition **plays at least two games** during the tournament week, and all games are held at the ESPN Wide World of Sports Complex. Champions are crowned in four categories for each of two divisions. Best of all, ESPN and ESPN2 showcase the games on a tape delay during the build-up to the NFL's Super Bowl.

The Cheer and Dance Championships follow a **similar structure**, with competition in two team-size categories, four age classifications, and three levels of skill.

Cheer and dance competitions are often held in The Milk House

Disney's All-Star Sports resort is popular with Pop Warner crowds

Maximizing My Experience

Since the Pop Warner Super Bowl and National Cheer and Dance Championships are **open to the public**, anyone who pays the entrance fee to the ESPN Wide World of Sports Complex ($13/ages 10 and up, $10/ages 3–9) can observe the events. If you love football or spirit squad competitions and will be near the complex, it is worth the price of admission to watch them. Who knows? You may even get a glimpse of a future NFL star like Emmitt Smith or Donovan McNabb, both of whom played Pop Warner football.

While there are many families accompanying their participants to Walt Disney World for the Super Bowl and Cheer and Dance Championships, most of their time is spent at the ESPN Wide World of Sports Complex competing in or training for the championships. Since early December is traditionally a slow time for the parks, most visitors will not notice any increase in park crowds.

President's Day Soccer Festival

Perhaps the highlight of the youth soccer events at Walt Disney World is the annual President's Day Soccer Festival. Disney invites teams from across the country to participate in this Florida Youth Soccer Association-sanctioned tournament. Friends and family can also attend the event at a cost of $25.50/ages 10 & up and $20.00/ages 3–9 for a length-of-event ticket or $13.00/ages 10 & up and $10.00/ages 3–9 daily. Visit http://espnwwos.disney.go.com/events/soccer/ presidents-day-soccer-festival/ for more information.

Competitive Running

Believe it or not, Walt Disney World offers a multitude of choices when it comes to competitive running, although "competitive running" might be a bit of a misnomer, as most participants are really only competing against themselves. Regardless, competitive running events at Walt Disney World remain popular with hard-core runners and Disney fans alike, and with **races held throughout the year**, Disney offers a race length for just about any skill level.

Over the past two years, Disney has added several new running events to its lineup and now offers seven races throughout the year. As each of these new events is met with an enthusiastic response, look for Disney to offer even more races.

Disney's Princess Half Marathon medals await finishers

What Can I Expect?

Running at Walt Disney World isn't just about winning the race, and Disney usually goes all out to **celebrate everyone who crosses the finish line**. Most races are capped by a party, and admission is included in cost of the race. Also included in the cost are medals for the finishers, refreshments during the race, commemorative race shirts, and programs.

Many of these races occur during Walt Disney World's **off-peak times** of year. Although crowds of supporters gather near certain places along the race route to cheer on participating friends and family, the impact on park crowds is usually minimal. As runners come along the race route, certain parts of the parks may experience closures or rerouting of traffic to accommodate the participants.

Those participating in the events should **plan on arriving early** and not touring the parks during the remainder of the day.

More information on every competitive running event held at Walt Disney World can be found at http://espnwwos.disney.go.com/sports/rundisney/.

Walt Disney World Marathon Weekend

The **crown jewel** of these competitive running events is the Walt Disney World Marathon. Held annually in early January, this event offers an exclusive opportunity to run through all four theme parks. The race is extremely popular with runners and is considered one of the best marathons in the country. Beginning at Epcot, runners follow the monorail line, pass through the Magic Kingdom, skirt the Magnolia and Palm golf courses, wind through the Animal Kingdom, make a U-turn at the ESPN Wide World of Sports Complex, hit Disney's Hollywood Studios, and then return to Epcot for the finish.

The **full marathon** costs $135/person, which includes race registration, an official race program, a commemorative race tech shirt, and entry to the post-race celebration and awards ceremony. All race finishers receive a medal, and those who finish within the allotted time of seven hours receive a certificate. Those registered for the event can also purchase a commemorative pin for $11.72.

Held the **day before the marathon**, the Walt Disney World Half Marathon is a 13-mile race that covers ground in the Magic Kingdom and Epcot. Popular with casual runners and Disney fans alike, this race allows participants to not only run down Main Street, U.S.A. like runners of the full marathon, but also get glimpses of a little backstage magic. Some brave souls use this race as a warm-up for the next day's full marathon, a combination known as Goofy's Race and a Half Challenge.

The cost for the **half marathon** is $135/person and includes race registration, an official program, a commemorative T-shirt, and entry to the post-race celebration and awards ceremony. All race finishers will receive a medal, and those who finish within the allotted time of 3 1/2 hours will receive a certificate. Those registered for the half marathon can also purchase a commemorative pin for $11.72.

Runners who participate in both races and register for Goofy's Race and a Half Challenge will receive a **medal**. The cost to participate in both events in 2011 is $310/person.

Those thinking about participating in these events should keep in mind that Disney does **strictly enforce a 16-minute-per-mile pace** for this race. Runners who do not make it to the checkpoints within the allotted time are transported via van to the finish line. While 16 minutes per mile doesn't sound very fast, it is a reasonable clip and does need to be maintained throughout the race.

Those looking for more information should visit http://espnwwos.disney.go.com/events/rundisney/wdw-marathon/.

Walt Disney World Marathon Weekend (continued)

If you are looking for a shorter run over Marathon Weekend, the Walt Disney World **Family Fun Run 5K** is just the ticket. For the past several years the race has been held at Disney's Animal Kingdom and dubbed The Circle of Life 5K. Runners begin and end near the front gate, traveling through Discovery Island and passing the Tree of Life, Kilimanjaro Safari, and Expedition Everest before heading backstage near DinoLand U.S.A.

The cost of the Family Fun Run 5K event is $45/person. All participants will receive a T-shirt, and finishers will receive a special medal. This race does have a 15-minute-per-mile requirement, so all participants should finish the race in about 45 minutes.

Kids aren't left out—the ESPN Wide World of Sports hosts **Disney's Family Fun Run Kids' Races** on Friday and Saturday of Marathon Weekend. Kids 8 and under (yes, even the infants can get in on the action here) participate in races grouped by age. The cost for this event is $10/child, which includes a special medal for each participant.

The Circle of Life 5K winds past the Tree of Life at Disney's Animal Kingdom

Champion 5K at ESPN The Weekend

This timed 5K run through Disney's Hollywood Studios coincides with ESPN The Weekend and benefits the **V Foundation for Cancer Research**. The race begins in the park's Television Lot and winds through the entire park before finishing back where it began. The cost is $45/person for the race only and $98 with a park ticket; prices increase to $50 and $103, respectively, after early registration ends. Participants receive an ESPN The Weekend T-shirt, a goody bag, a personalized race bib, and a finisher's medal. Additional theme park tickets for friends and family cost $53/person.

Kid races are held after the conclusion of 5K, and the $10 registration fee includes a race bib, shirt, and finisher's medal. See http://espnwwos.disney.go.com/events/rundisney/espn-5k/ for more information.

Disney's Princess Half Marathon Weekend

While the Minnie Marathon is no more, Disney's Princess Half Marathon has taken its place. Be warned, this race isn't for the faint of heart or those wearing glass slippers, it is the real deal—a 13.1-mile half marathon. Held in late February, this race is expected to become **one of the top women's endurance events** in the country! Like the half marathon in January, this race does carry a 16-minute mile requirement, so participants will want to ensure they're ready to run.

The race begins at Spaceship Earth in Epcot, heads to the Magic Kingdom and through Cinderella Castle, and finishes in Epcot. Each runner receives a **commemorative tech shirt**, a goody bag, event transportation from select resort hotels, a personalized bib, on-course refreshments and Disney entertainment, post-race refreshments, and access to a family reunion area with characters and live entertainment. The cost for this event is $120/person.

The **Royal Family 5K Run** is held on the same weekend. Participants circle the World Showcase before ending at Spaceship Earth. This race is open to the entire family, and everyone who either walks or runs will receive a medal! Additionally, runners will receive a personalized bib, a goody bag, and post race refreshments. The entry fee is $45, or $50 for the Stroller Division.

Disney also offers **Royal Family Kids' Races** during the Princess Marathon Weekend. Races range from a 100-meter dash for 1- to 3-year-olds to an 800-meter dash for 9- to 11-year-olds, and there's a Diaper Dash for crawlers under 12 months. Registrants receive a personalized bib, a commemorative kids T-shirt, and a finisher's medallion. The entry fee is $10.

Check out http://espnwwos.disney.go.com/events/rundisney/princess-half-marathon/ for more information.

Expedition Everest Challenge

The newest race at Walt Disney World is also the most unusual. Held in late September at Disney's Animal Kingdom, this team-based competition is one part 5K race, one part obstacle course, and **one part scavenger hunt**. The competition culminates with an exclusive after-hours party for you and your teammates. Lest you think this is less competitive than other events at Walt Disney World, this race does have a 15-minute per mile requirement for the 5K and 2 1/2-hour time limit for the entire competition.

Participants receive admission to one theme park for a day, a Champion tech shirt, and admission to the aforementioned after-hours party at Disney's Animal Kingdom. Those who finish also receive a **commemorative medal**. Cost for the event is $195 for teams of two or $100/person. Visit http://espnwwos.disney.go.com/events/rundisney/expedition-everest-challenge/ for more information.

Wine & Dine Half Marathon Weekend

To celebrate the 15th annual Epcot International Food & Wine Festival, Disney introduced an enhanced endurance race to replace Disney's Race for the Taste 10K & 3K. Held the first weekend in October, the new event features a half marathon, new kids' races, and the **5K Mickey's Halloween Family Fun Run**. The 10K race begins with a ceremonial toast at the ESPN Wide World of Sports Complex and then takes participants through Disney's Hollywood Studios en route to the finish line at Epcot. The 5K race begins and ends in the Magic Kingdom and is themed to the fun of Halloween at the park. Participants are encouraged to race in costume, making this one to be enjoyed by the whole family. As the only 5K race to be held entirely in the Magic Kingdom, this new race offers a unique experience in addition to a "trick or treat" bag of goodies at the end.

The cost is $135/person for the half marathon, which includes access to an exclusive after-race party. The cost for Mickey's Halloween Family Fun 5K is $53.95/person 10 and up and includes admission to Mickey's Not So Scary Halloween Party the next day. **Special ChEAR Squad packages** are available for spectators at Silver ($35/person) and Gold ($50) levels. The Silver package includes a special bag, noisemaker, and T-shirt, while the Gold package adds reserved viewing locations at the starting and finish lines, along with special transportation to the viewing locations. Tickets for spectators are available by calling 407-WDW-IRUN.

Check out http://espnwwos.disney.go.com/events/rundisney/wine-and-dine-half-marathon/ for more information.

© Patrick Johnson

Registration for Mickey's Halloween Family Fun Run includes admission to Mickey's Not-So-Scary Halloween Party the next day!

Other Endurance Events

If running across Walt Disney World isn't enough of a challenge, why not toss in some **biking and swimming too?**

Columbia Muddy Buddy Ride & Run

The Muddy Buddy series is a six- to seven-mile trail-running and mountain biking adventure complete with **obstacles and a mud pit**! Teams of two "leapfrog" through a course that winds around the ESPN Wide World of Sports Complex, running and swapping off riding a single bike. Afterward, participants can relax at the Muddy Buddy BBQ, featuring a raffle and awards ceremony, and enjoy two free beers in the Muddy Buddy Beer Garden. The cost is $165 per team, and participants receive a T-shirt, a goody bag, and chances to win the raffle and a Land Rover Driving School Experience.

The Mini Muddy Buddy offers kids ages 4-12 the chance to run their very own **obstacle course** with mud pit. Registration costs $15, and participants receive a bib, a T-shirt, and a finisher medal. Half the proceeds go to the Challenged Athletes Foundation. More information is available at http://www.muddybuddy.com/.

Florida Ironman 70.3 Triathlon

Held each **May**, the Florida Ironman 70.3 triathlon consists of a 1.2-mile swim, a 56-mile bike ride, and a 13.1-mile run. This competition also includes a weekend expo and a race for the kids. The cost is $275/person. Because this is not an official Disney event but part of the Ford Ironman Series, registration lacks many of the extras the other Walt Disney World competitions have. More information is available at http://www.floridahalfironman.com/.

An Ironman Triathlon swim

Danskin Orlando Triathlon

Just in time for Mother's Day, Danskin sponsors one of two triathlons held on Disney property **exclusively for women**. May's Danskin Orlando Triathlon, which is also part of the USA Triathlon series, consists of a quarter-mile swim in Seven Seas Lagoon, a 9-mile bike ride on the resort's traffic-controlled roads, and a 2-mile run through the Magic Kingdom.

© Akleos

Although the event is held at Walt Disney World, it lacks the extras of official Disney races and is strictly a competitive event. The cost for this event is $90/person or $150/team during early registration, and

Fort Wilderness hosts many triathlons

$95 or $165 thereafter. You will require a $10 one-day membership to the USA Triathlon organization for liability and insurance. More information is available at http://www.danskinwomenstri.com/.

IronKids Orlando

Held in May, the IronKids Orlando event gives **children ages 6-15** the chance to participate in their own version of a triathalon at Fort Wilderness Resort. The $50 registration fee includes an "IronKids Finisher" T-shirt, a goodie bag, and a K-dot finisher medal. Up to two additional family members may register at the discounted rate of $35 each. More information is available at http://www.ironkids.com/Events/IronKids_Orlando.htm.

Trek Women Triathlon Series

The Trek Women's Triathlon Series is held at Fort Wilderness in **September**. Like the Danskin Orlando Triathalon, it is **not an official Disney event**. The course features a half-mile swim, a 12-mile bike ride, and a 3.1-mile run. The entry fee is $75/person ($80 on the day of the event) or $145/relay team ($160 on the day of the event), plus a $10 one-day membership to USA Triathlon. For more information, check out http://www.trekwomenstriathlonseries.com/.

🔱 Orlando International Dragon Boat Festival

At Disney, dragons aren't just the little purple ones of our imagination anymore: In mid-October you can see dozens of them at the annual Orlando International Dragon Boat Festival, a showcase of a team paddling sport that originated in China more than 2,000 years ago. Held at Downtown Disney, this event boasts world-class competition among teams of 20 paddlers and one steersperson, who are accompanied on their boat by a drummer and up to four alternates. Admission is free for spectators, with team pricing ranging from $1,000–$1,850 depending on division and when you register. Visit http://www.gwndragonboat.com for more information.

Children's Miracle Network Classic

While baseball and football players come to Walt Disney World for preseason training camps, professional golfers on the **PGA Tour** come to the resort not to train but to compete. Every year in mid-November, the best golfers showcase their skills on Disney's Magnolia and Palm competition golf courses in the Children's Miracle Network Classic (formerly called the FUNAI Classic), providing an opportunity for golf fans to watch their favorite players compete for a tour championship.

For four decades, the PGA has ended its fall tour with a stop at Walt Disney World. Golfers especially enjoy this, as it allows them an opportunity to bring their families along and enjoy a little time off before the main tour begins again in January. Many of the **top names in the sport**, like Tiger Woods, Vijay Singh, and Davis Love III, have competed in and won this tournament.

The tournament is played at the **Magnolia and Palm golf courses**, located near Disney's Magic Kingdom. Practice rounds take place on Monday, Tuesday, and Wednesday of the tournament week. Thursday and Friday feature the opening rounds of the PGA stroke-play tournament and offer fans the opportunity to play along at one of the rare PGA Tour Pro-Am events. Saturday and Sunday feature the last days of the tournament, with the winner crowned late Sunday afternoon.

The Pro-Am is a great chance for the **serious amateur** to play with some favorite golfers. While this experience isn't cheap (think $10,000), the package does include two member badges and four guest badges, special access to the private hospitality tent for food and beverages, courtesy car transportation during the event, and 25 weekly tournament tickets to give to family and friends. Other perks include eight days of unlimited golf for two, an annual Miracle Makers Club golf membership, 12 one-day Park Hopper tickets, and six 10-day Magic Your Way theme park tickets.

If your golf game isn't quite up to par with the big guys', multiple options exist for observing the action. Fans can choose from **single-day tickets** ($10/person) or a weeklong pass for the serious fan ($20/person). Kids also get in on the action at the Kid's Zone tent. Youngsters can improve their golf games with hands-on exhibits and interactive demos, including video games. Admission to the Kid's Zone is free with a paid adult tournament ticket.

In addition to the tournament itself, golf fans can enjoy either the Osprey Ridge course near Fort Wilderness or the nine-hole Oak Trail course near the tournament courses. Both offer **tournament-style play** for golf enthusiasts. Costs for the Osprey Ridge course are $89/person Monday-Friday and $99/person Friday-Sunday for resort guests. Day visitors pay $104/person Monday-Friday and $114/person Friday-Sunday. Discounts are available after either 2 pm or 3 pm, depending on season. The Oak Trail nine-hole walking course is $38/ages 18 & up and $20/ages 17 & under, and this course offers a replay rate of 50% off the regular rates.

Other Sporting Events

In addition to myriad participatory sports activities, Walt Disney World offers even more **spectator sports and tournaments**. Aside from the ones already mentioned in this chapter, the ESPN Wide World of Sports Complex hosts several tournaments for amateur competitors from around the world. Best of all, these tournaments occur throughout the year, so no matter when you go, you're certain to find one to see. For information on any of these events, visit http://espnwwos.disney.go.com/.

Martial Arts
Believe it or not, the ESPN Wide World of Sports Complex hosts **two competitive martial arts tournaments**. Held in July, the USA Judo National Junior Olympics is part of the selection process for junior teams to participate in international competitions. Disney's Martial Arts Festival occurs in October. Covering a multitude of martial arts, this festival brings more than 1,200 athletes and coaches to the resort.

Volleyball
With **two tournaments** each year, the ESPN Wide World of Sports Complex welcomes hundreds of volleyball players, coaches, and fans. In late March, the resort hosts the Disney Volleyball Classic, an open tournament offering competition in four different age categories. Early September brings the KSA Fall Classic Volleyball Tournament & Scrimmages.

Soccer
Walt Disney World hosts **10 annual tournaments** for the most popular sport in the world. One of the highlights is Disney's President's Day Soccer Festival, which features tournaments for boys and girls in mid-February. In November, Disney hosts the Junior Soccer Showcase for players under the age of 14. In May, Disney's Memorial Day Soccer Shootout brings more than 300 teams to the resort for the three-day weekend.

Softball & Baseball
As if hosting the Atlanta Braves' spring training weren't enough, Champion Stadium at the ESPN Wide World of Sports also offers lots of bat-and-ball action in **17 tournaments and training seminars**. Fast or slow pitch, men's, women's, or co-ed, Disney has your bases covered with tournaments for all ages and teams. And to get your team ready for competition, a trip to Disney's Softball Spring Training will pay big dividends later in the season!

Basketball
If you prefer a different sort of round ball, Disney hosts **several basketball tournaments**, including the AAU Nationals for both boys' and girls' teams. With the younger kids taking the court in April and the older kids competing in the summer, the AAU Nationals offer basketball fans the chance to watch future stars shoot for a national championship. March Madness fanatics should note that the road to the Final Four really begins in November with the Old Spice Classic, which is held each year at the ESPN Wide World of Sports Complex. This event is televised nationally on the ESPN family of networks.

Chapter 5
Holidays

Disney does a great job of creating reasons to come to Walt Disney World, but The Mouse is also fantastic at **highlighting days and seasons** that the rest of the world celebrates. Since many people look for ways to celebrate those holidays at the resort, Disney obliges with special parties, parades, fireworks, and decorations. Whether it is a major holiday like Christmas or a minor one like Groundhog Day, Disney is quick to remind us with appropriate events, merchandise, and decorations.

© MediaMarx, Inc.

Mickey's Jingle Jungle Parade

While just about any special day qualifies as a holiday when you're at Walt Disney World, this chapter focuses on the **major national holidays**. The parks don't break out the decorations and fireworks for, say, Veterans Day the way they do for Independence Day. However, there are often special remembrances on those days, so it doesn't hurt to ask Guest Relations if anything is going on during holidays that don't merit a merchandising tie-in.

The key to celebrating a holiday at Walt Disney World is **planning**. Holidays usually mean larger crowds and jam-packed restaurants. Since food is a large part

© Stephanie Fieldstad

Mickey's Very Merry Christmas Party

of many celebrations, guests should plan dining reservations months in advance. Although Disney guarantees park entry for resort hotel guests, there is no guarantee which park you'll be allowed to enter. If you want to be in Epcot on New Year's Eve, plan on arriving early and spending the day in the park.

With that in mind, let's trim the tree and light the Roman candles, because it's time to celebrate some of the **most wonderful times of the year!**

Christmas at Walt Disney World

If there is one time of year that Mickey and his pals make every effort to impress, it has to be the **winter holiday season**, when so many people celebrate. From Hanukkah to Christmas to New Year's, this is one of the most magical times of the year at Walt Disney World.

People from around the globe are drawn to the resort to experience this magic firsthand. In fact, the week between Christmas and New Year's Day is consistently the **busiest of the entire year**. Despite the crowds, many families find that spending the holiday season at Walt Disney World is something they wouldn't exchange for the world.

What Can I Expect?

While the parks and resort hotels look terrific throughout the year, the special decorations at this time of year are nothing short of **spectacular**. Each area of each park is decorated in a unique way that reflects the character of the park or land and the spirit of the holidays. But decorations are only the beginning of the celebration.

With a gigantic Christmas tree in Town Square, it's hard not to get into the holiday spirit the moment you enter the **Magic Kingdom**. The holidays also bring Mickey's Very Merry Christmas Party (see page 23) and its special fireworks, which can also be seen during regular park hours in the week around Christmas Day (from just before Christmas until New Year's Day). Likewise, the daily parade receives a holiday makeover that is the focus of the nationally televised Walt Disney World Christmas Day Parade. But if you are looking forward to experiencing the parade live, you'll have to make plans to enjoy it sometime other than Christmas morning—the parade is usually filmed during the first weekend in December.

Over at **Epcot**, the World Showcase gives guests a glimpse into holiday traditions around the world. Each pavilion features storytellers who share the ways people in their country celebrate. The IllumiNations: Reflections of Earth fireworks show also receives a holiday makeover, with a special ending that celebrates the season. And Mickey and his friends conduct a tree-lighting ceremony each night near the entrance to the World Showcase.

Perhaps the most magical holiday activity at Epcot is the retelling of the Christmas story in the **Candlelight Processional**. Celebrity narrators are accompanied by a 50-piece orchestra and a mass choir performing specially arranged songs that complement the story. This incredibly popular show is performed three times each night before capacity crowds. The narrators change every year, and previous celebrity narrators include Steven Curtis Chapman, Gary Sinise, Kirk Cameron, and Neil Patrick Harris. Check http://allears.net/tp/h_cpfaq.htm for the schedule.

Many people choose add a **Candlelight Lunch or Dinner Package** to their Candlelight Processional experience. The package includes a buffet or three-course meal at one of Epcot's restaurants, reserved seating for Candlelight Processional, and entrance into a reserved viewing area for the IllumiNations: Reflections of Earth fireworks show.

Since seating for the Processional is often scarce, lines are long, and most guests will eat prior to attending the show, this option can be attractive. Prices depend on the restaurant and type of meal you select: lunch costs $32.99–$51.99/adults and $12.99–$17.99/child, while dinner costs $46.99–$61.99/adult and $15.99–$23.99/child. Guests receive a badge from their server at the time of their meal and should arrive at America Gardens Theater at least 15 minutes prior to the show—or earlier for the best seats. Call 407-WDW-DINE for reservations and additional information.

Disney's Hollywood Studios hosts one of the most legendary displays of holiday lights in the world, the Osborne Family Spectacle of Dancing Lights presented by Sylvania. After neighbors in Jennings Osborne's Arkansas hometown complained about the crowds drawn to the spectacular holiday light displays on and around his house, the courts ordered Osborne to take the lights down. Disney stepped in and offered to

© LFDawson

Osborne Family Spectacle of Lights

host the light show each Christmas on the streets of Disney's Hollywood Studios. Since its debut in 1995, the display has become one of Walt Disney World's most popular holiday happenings.

Disney's Animal Kingdom gets its share of holiday cheer too. The daily parade is transformed into Mickey's Jingle Jungle Parade, Santa Goofy holds court at his Wild Wonderland, and strolling carolers perform in Camp Minnie-Mickey and the Oasis.

The theme parks aren't the only place to get into holi4ay spirit. The **resort hotels** also go all-out to bring guests holiday cheer. While each resort has incredible decorations worthy of a touring day themselves, one of the perennial favorites is the gingerbread house at Disney's Grand Floridian Resort & Spa. This is not your average gingerbread house—it's a full-size cottage featuring a walk-in gift shop in the back selling smaller versions of this sweet house. The lobbies of the other Deluxe resorts feature their own holiday-themed food sculptures.

The closer it gets to the holidays, the more the resorts get into the spirit, with some featuring carolers and serving hot chocolate in their lobbies. If a **sleigh ride** sounds like fun, a trip over to Disney's Wilderness Lodge is in order. This rustic retreat offers sleigh rides daily throughout the month of December for groups of up to four adults or two adults and three children, at a cost of $60/sleigh.

Many of the theme park **restaurants** feature special holiday meals, especially those in Epcot's World Showcase, where the countries often offer traditional holiday food. Be warned, however, that these meals are extremely popular and guests should make dining reservations as early as possible.

Maximizing My Experience

While any trip to Walt Disney World requires planning, visiting during the winter holidays requires a **serious touring plan**. Large crowds can limit your choices if you don't plan ahead. Try to make dining reservations as soon as possible to ensure the widest variety of choices. If you are visiting on Christmas Day, consider dining at Liberty Tree Tavern in the Magic Kingdom for a traditional holiday meal, or head over to Epcot and enjoy a Christmas feast in your ancestors' native land.

Gingerbread display at the BoardWalk Resort

Shopping is synonymous with the holidays for many people, and Disney offers several specialty stores to help you take a bit of the magic back with you. Disney's Days of Christmas, located at Downtown Disney, offers a wide selection of unique Disney-themed holiday merchandise. If you want to pick something up in the Magic Kingdom, be sure to visit Ye Olde Christmas Shoppe in Liberty Square. And if you need a pickle for your Tannenbaum, the shops in Epcot's Germany pavilion offer many traditional tree ornaments.

Finally, all visitors should make time to tour the entire resort to enjoy the **decorations**. Venturing beyond the parks to the hotel lobbies or Downtown Disney gives guests an opportunity to experience some Disney magic for little more than the time it takes to venture from place to place. Combining a trip to a resort hotel for a meal with some time to enjoy the decorations gives guests a great opportunity to capture some holiday magic Disney-style.

The Grand Floridian at Christmas

Wilderness Lodge at Christmas

Valentine's Day at Walt Disney World

Walt Disney World offers many opportunities for couples to celebrate the most romantic day of the year. Aside from the occasional pin and merchandise push, Walt Disney World has few official commemorations of Valentine's Day, but the resort offers myriad **romantic options** for lovebirds of all ages.

Many of the **restaurants** on property are extremely romantic, with popular choices such as Le Cellier and Victoria & Albert's among the best. If you plan to dine at any Walt Disney World restaurant on Valentine's Day, be sure to make your dining reservations early, lest you find yourself chowing down with a polka band or crunching on chicken strips outside of Space Mountain (unless you find that romantic!). At the Deluxe resort hotels,

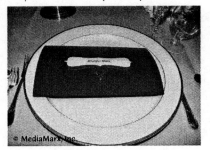

Personalized menu at Victoria & Albert's

Disney's Private Dining can help you arrange everything from a simple meal on your balcony to a multicourse feast served on the beach by your own butler! Call the main number for your resort and ask to speak with Private Dining for more information.

Romance isn't limited to culinary delights. Why not grab a couple of glasses of Champagne from Epcot's France pavilion and enjoy the IllumiNations: Reflections of Earth fireworks show? For $275 and up, you may also charter a fireworks cruise during IllumiNations or the Magic Kingdom's Wishes show (and take along up to 10-12 of your friends!). The mahogany runabout Breathless II is available to charter for $320 during IllumiNations, and daytime cruises cost $102 per half hour. Call 407-WDW-PLAY for more information.

Other romantic activities include the couples' spa treatments at Disney's Grand Floridian Spa ($275-$375/couple) and **carriage rides** at Port Orleans Riverside Resort ($35).

For more information about these experiences and **additional ideas** for creating romance at Walt Disney World, check out the "Honeymoons & Anniversaries at Walt Disney World" chapter of the *PassPorter's Disney Weddings & Honeymoons* guidebook.

Easter at Walt Disney World

Easter brings a celebration that encompasses both the **secular and the sacred** aspects of the holiday. The Contemporary Resort hosts Protestant and Roman Catholic services in the Fantasia Ballroom on Easter Sunday. Traditionally, the services start at 8:00 am, with the Roman Catholic Mass first, then the Protestant service at 9:00 am. The morning ends with a second Mass at 10:15 am.

Most **resorts** host egg hunts and other Easter activities, ranging from Bunny Bingo to diving for eggs. These are usually free or carry a nominal charge. The one exception is also one of the more exotic options: Animal Kingdom Lodge guests can decorate ostrich eggs when they make a $25 donation to the Disney Wildlife Conservation Fund. One thing to keep in mind, however, is that these activities are available only to resort guests and are not open to guests from other resort hotels or those staying outside the Walt Disney World Resort.

Many people choose to celebrate Easter with **brunch**. Disney accommodates guests by extending the hours at popular restaurants like Chef Mickey's and the Crystal Palace. It is important to remember that, as with all holidays, these meals are very popular. Be sure to make dining reservations early to avoid disappointment.

If the little ones insist that Mickey is no substitute for the **Easter Bunny**, don't despair! The week leading up to Easter Sunday finds the popular rabbit and his missus meeting and greeting guests in the Tour Guide Garden at the Magic Kingdom. This is also a great opportunity to get a shot of the whole family, as Disney PhotoPass photographers are on hand to capture the moment on film.

Mother's Day at Walt Disney World

Brunch is perhaps the most popular way to celebrate moms, and there are usually several options at Walt Disney World. In 2010, Tables In Wonderland offered its members a meal in the "Under the Sea Garden"—a special champagne brunch at the Living Seas Salon in Epcot. Two seatings were offered, and the price was $95/person. Tables In Wonderland is a dining discount club for Walt Disney World annual passholders and Florida residents. For information on future events and or to join, call (407) 566-5858.

Downtown Disney also gets into the act, with restaurants like Fulton's Crab House, Portobello, and Wolfgang Puck Grand Cafe and Dining Room offering special Mother's Day menus.

Father's Day at Walt Disney World

Although Disney doesn't offer any official Father's Day events, dads have a wide variety of options for **celebrating their special day**. Four championship courses offer plenty of fun for golfing dads, while a fishing expedition on Bay Lake or another Walt Disney World waterway makes a great gift for the sportsman. And what dad doesn't like to eat? Options range from a visit to the ESPN Zone for the sports lover to fine dining at Yachtsman Steakhouse for the connoisseur.

Fourth of July at Walt Disney World

One of the most explosive days of the year, America's Independence Day brings **special fireworks and extended park hours** to accommodate the large crowds at Walt Disney World. Most notably, the classic show Fantasy in the Sky replaces Wishes for two nights at the Magic Kingdom. In the past, the skies over Disney's Hollywood Studios lit up with the Sorcery in the Sky fireworks, although in 2007 the park offered different special fireworks. Additional showings of regular nighttime shows like Fantasmic! and SpectroMagic also entertain the crowds, and guests who leave the parks and head to Pleasure Island will see not only fireworks but live entertainment as well.

Guests may also want to visit two of the most **patriotic attractions** at Walt Disney World. The Hall of Presidents at the Magic Kingdom highlights the men who have led the United States, while the American Adventure at Epcot tells the story of the "everyman" and his equally important part in shaping the nation. Epcot visitors can add on a visit to the National Treasures exhibit at the American Adventure pavilion, which features such artifacts as Abraham Lincoln's hat and Thomas Edison's phonograph.

Halloween at Walt Disney World

While Mickey's Not-So-Scary Halloween Party (see page 21) gets all the headlines, **Pleasure Island and Downtown Disney** also get into the action. Various shops offer trick-or-treaters special surprises, with treat bags available free at the World of Disney store and other select merchants. The new Mickey's Halloween Fun Run 5K adds to the festivities at the Magic Kingdom. However, aside from seasonal decorations around the resort, these are the only Halloween offerings at Walt Disney World.

Thanksgiving at Walt Disney World

At Walt Disney World, Thanksgiving often gets lost in the shuffle between Halloween and Christmas. Aside from **extended hours and special menus** at certain restaurants, little else is planned since Disney's Christmas season is in full swing by the time Thanksgiving Day arrives. With their traditional fare, eateries like Garden Grill in Epcot and Liberty Tree Tavern in the Magic Kingdom are among the most popular Thanksgiving dining options.

Restaurants with special Thanksgiving menus generally include the following: **Cinderella's Royal Table** offers a pre-plated traditional turkey feast, **Crystal Palace** features Thanksgiving favorites at all three meals, **Liberty Tree Tavern** serves up a lunch buffet and dinner, and **Tony's Town Square** has a la carte menu with traditional Thanksgiving dishes with an Italian flair. Over at Epcot, **Garden Grill** offers an all-you-care-to-eat turkey and steak feast at dinner.

Other restaurants with special Thanksgiving menus may include: Biergarten, Le Cellier, Rose and Crown, '50s Prime Time Cafe, Hollywood Brown Derby, Hollywood & Vine, End Zone Food Court, Boma, Jiko, Cape May Cafe, Flying Fish Cafe, Shutters, California Grill, Chef Mickey's, The Wave, Mickey's Backyard BBQ, Trail's End, 1900 Park Fare, Citricos, Grand Floridian Cafe, Narcoossee's, Victoria & Albert's, Olivia's, 'Ohana, Kona Cafe, Spirit of Aloha, Boatwright's, Turf Club Grill, Artist Point, Whispering Canyon Cafe, Yacht Club Galley, Yachtsman Steakhouse, Portobello Yacht Club, Raglan Road, Wolfgang Puck's, and Fulton's Crab House.

New Year's Eve at Walt Disney World

New Year's Eve is perhaps the **most popular day** to be in the parks, and celebrating at Walt Disney World is a great way to ring in the New Year. The party brings special fireworks and parades, along with extended park hours. In fact, thanks to Extra Magic Hours, guests can ring in the New Year by spending 37 of the last 41 hours of the old year in the Magic Kingdom!

Downtown Disney and the BoardWalk also get into the act. A special version of Cirque du Soleil's *La Nouba* on New Year's Eve ($67-$133/ages 10 and up, $54-$105/ages 3-9) includes a souvenir program, a Champagne toast, and a special ending. Atlantic Dance Hall holds a party as well, with tickets ($10) on sale the day of the event. The venue offers a buffet and music to ring in the New Year!

New Year's Eve is arguably the most crowded time of the year at Walt Disney World. Guests will want to **plan accordingly** to make sure they are where they want to be when the clock strikes twelve. Unlike Cinderella, you may not have your ride turn into a pumpkin, but you just might find yourself locked out of the Magic Kingdom if you don't arrive early and make reservations for dining or special activities well in advance.

© Stephanie Fieldstad

A special IllumiNations: Reflections of Earth

Other Holidays at Walt Disney World

Many **other days** hold significance for people from around the world, such as Bastille Day in France or Cinco de Mayo in Mexico. Epcot's World Showcase often celebrates these days in the appropriate pavilions, allowing guests an additional opportunity to experience the culture of other countries. Raglan Road restaurant at Downtown Disney is a popular place to celebrate St. Patrick's Day, as one might expect. And some parks celebrate certain holidays when they tie in with the theme of the park, like Disney's Animal Kingdom and Earth Day. More information about these holidays can be found at Guest Relations or your hotel's Concierge desk. If you like to know before you go, check the PassPorter web site (http://www.passporter.com) or All Ears Net (http://www.allears.net).

Flag ceremony on Main Street, U.S.A. on September 11

Chapter 6
Your Special Day

Although 2009's year-long celebration asking guests, "What will you celebrate?" has ended, Walt Disney World still ranks among the most popular places for people to **mark important life milestones**. Guests celebrate birthdays, anniversaries, graduations, and more every day. Let's look at how you and yours can take a momentous occasion and make it unforgettable with a visit to Walt Disney World.

Making It Known

Walt Disney World is a magical place, and cast members really go out of their way to **sprinkle your special day with even more pixie dust**. Many guests report receiving complimentary desserts, gifts in their hotel rooms, invitations to participate in parades and fireworks shows, and dozens of other fun treats from cast members who found out they were celebrating a special occasion. The trick is to let cast members know that you are celebrating, and Disney makes it easy to do with complimentary buttons for numerous special occasions.

Available from any Guest Relations location in the Disney parks, these buttons allow guests to announce **birthdays, anniversaries, weddings, first visits,** and more. Guests report receiving many perks when wearing these buttons, ranging from congratulations to special desserts. Just remember: You may receive that extra pixie dust, but nothing can guarantee you will. The best approach is to enjoy your special day with no expectation of perks. Still, you'll find that Disney cast members do a great job of recognizing those wearing these buttons because they assume those guests want some additional magic.

It also helps to **mention your special occasion** to your travel agent or Disney's Central Reservations Office when booking your trip. Likewise, it wouldn't hurt to mention your celebration when checking in to your resort to make sure the cast members there know. Even if you don't want a big deal made at every meal, there is a good chance that if you tell someone ahead of time, special gifts like balloons or autograph cards from a certain mouse will magically appear in your room while you are out.

Mentioning the occasion to any **cast members** you meet usually nets great results. Remember, Disney wants to make your day special so you'll visit the resort again to celebrate. By sharing your occasion with cast members, you'll stand a greater chance of witnessing some extra magic to enhance your special day.

Birthdays, Graduations, and More!

What does a person do to make a birthday or other special occasion even more special? **Hold a party** for a few friends at Walt Disney World! While Disney offers myriad possibilities for special parties, from fireworks cruises to quinceañeras, we focus on a few options that guests may not know about. It is important to remember that almost anything is possible for the right price, and guests should contact 407-WDW-BDAY for more information about these and other possibilities for celebrating that special day. Disney markets many of these as birthday parties, but other celebrations are welcome.

Younger guests will love the special Never Land Club party at the Polynesian Resort. For $30/child (minimum of 10 children), your group will receive exclusive access to the club for two hours, a meal of pizza or chicken strips, party games, cake, crafts, and other activities all based on one of five themes: sports, luau, princess, pirate, and Mickey/Minnie. For $70/child, your group receives the basic package plus a visit from a character who fits the party's theme.

The **Pirate and Pals Fireworks Voyage**, which was previously open only to Grand Gatherings groups, is now available to all. Check out page 66 for more information.

You can **add a cake to a table-service restaurant meal** by calling the Cake Ordering Hotline at 407-827-2253 at least 48 hours in advance. These customized birthday cakes vary in price depending on how elaborate the design is. Most table-service restaurants also keep on hand 6-inch cakes in either vanilla or chocolate. These cost $21 and can be requested at the podium when you arrive for your meal.

Guests staying at a Deluxe Disney resort hotel can call Private Dining at their resort to order **a cake for room delivery**. If your resort does not have room service, you may be able to purchase 6-inch chocolate or vanilla cakes in the refrigerated case at the food court.

The **BoardWalk Bakery** at BoardWalk Inn Resort is the only bakery on property that will let you order a custom cake to pick up. Call the resort at 407-939-5100 and ask to speak with someone in the bakery for more information. Fancier cakes require at least one week's notice, but basic options can be arranged 48 hours in advance.

Birthday cake at Restaurant Akershus

Engagements, Weddings, & Anniversaries

For many people, Walt Disney World is the ideal place to **propose**, and there are many wonderful ways to do this, ranging from official engagement packages to spur-of-the-moment declarations in a meaningful area of a park or resort. Cinderella's Royal Table offers a special engagement package that includes preferred seating, a meal, toasting flutes, and the surprise presentation of your engagement ring inside a glass slipper. For full details, call 407-824-4477 or send an e-mail to wdwcrtsspecialevents@email.disney.com. There are plenty of other romantic ways—and places—to pop the question at Walt Disney World for low or no cost. It never hurts to ask for help from cast members. They may be able to help you pull off a surprise or arrange to bring a PhotoPass photographer along to capture the moment. And if you aren't sure where to start, try asking for ideas on the PassPorter community message boards at http://www.passporterboards.com. Look for our special Disney for Romance forum!

Jennifer and Dave Marx on their wedding day at the Grand Floridian

If you wish to celebrate by renewing your vows or to say them for the first time, Walt Disney World offers complete **wedding ceremonies**, ranging from casual to formal. Visit the official Disney Weddings web site at http://www.disneyweddings.com for more information, or check out *PassPorter's Disney Weddings & Honeymoons*, a comprehensive guide and bridal organizer for planning weddings, vow renewals, and commitment ceremonies at Walt Disney World.

Guests looking for an **intimate way to celebrate anniversaries or honeymoons** may want to check out the ideas on Disney's honeymoon web site, http://www.disneyhoneymoons.com, or read the "Honeymoons & Anniversaries at Walt Disney World" chapter of *PassPorter's Disney Weddings & Honeymoons*.

A romantic meal at Victoria & Albert's would be a memorable part of your special day. The only Disney eatery to earn four stars from the prestigious Mobil Travel Guide, Victoria & Albert's features elegant Victorian décor, a harpist, personalized menus, and a rose for each lady. Another idea is to enlist the aid of the pixies at Gifts of a Lifetime (http://giftsofalifetime.com), who give guests the opportunity to make a special moment more magical and possibly capture it on film. This unique service offers gifts ranging from bouquets or personalized Disney items to customized in-park scavenger hunts. The Disney Florist (http://www.disneyflorist.com) will deliver a wide variety of special gifts and flowers to your resort room. Prices range from $40 for a flower arrangement to $390 for a romantic package of bath products and monogrammed Mickey towels.

Grand Gatherings

Guests wanting something beyond the standard party can explore the many options that Disney offers guests as part of the **Grand Gatherings program for groups** of eight or more. Looking to add international flair to your special day?

Head over to Epcot for the **International Dinner and IllumiNations Dessert Reception**. Held in the Odyssey Center, the dinner offers guests international dishes under the watchful eye of host Auntie Roz. After a delicious meal, guests head to a reserved viewing area to enjoy dessert and the IllumiNations: Reflections of Earth fireworks show. Believe it or not, this celebration isn't only for the high rollers—the cost is $69.99-$73.99/ages 10 and up and $33.99-$35.99/ages 3-9; theme park admission is required.

For the same price, guests can head over to Disney's Animal Kingdom and enjoy the **Safari Celebration Dinner**. After a private tour of Kilimanjaro Safaris, partygoers move to the Tusker House restaurant for an all-you-can-eat feast of African-style dishes. Following the meal, guests get an up-close look at wildlife in the restaurant courtyard and the opportunity to get autographs from special Disney characters!

If breakfast is more your thing, the **Good Morning Character Breakfast** is perfect for you! Held at Tony's Town Square Restaurant in the Magic Kingdom, this unique character experience offers an all-you-can-eat breakfast as Tony, Mickey, and their friends mingle with guests. After breakfast, guests enjoy reserved seating at the next available showing of Mickey's PhilharMagic! Prices are $34.99-$38.99/ages 10 and up and $20.99-$22.99/ages 3-9, depending on the season.

Alternatively, you can skip the meal and set sail from the Contemporary Resort on the **Pirate and Pals Fireworks Voyage**. After a snack, board your own private pirate ship with Captain Hook and Mr. Smee for a night of fireworks, the Electrical Water Pageant, songs, trivia, and more! As you sail back to the harbor, you'll hear the story of Peter Pan. Upon your return, you'll find the kid who doesn't want to grow up waiting for you at the dock for autographs and pictures! Prices are $53.99/ages 10 and up and $30.99 ages 3-9.

If these options don't appeal to you, Disney offers other **unique opportunities** for groups. Private dessert-party showings of Fantasmic! or cruises for up-close viewing of IllumiNations: Reflections of Earth just scratch the surface of what Disney offers. And while only major corporations have rented an entire theme park, it is certainly possible for anyone. Remember, just about anything can happen at Disney for the right price.

It's important to remember that **reservations are required** for these events, ranging from at least three days to as many as 180 days in advance. Disney requires full payment 45 days in advance or at the time of the reservation, and the payment is nonrefundable. To schedule any of these activities or to inquire about other celebration options, call 407-WDW-MAGIC or visit http://www.disneyworld.com/magicalgatherings.

The Party Never Ends!

While you've reached the end of this book, we know there's still **more to share** about Disney's wonderful festivals and celebrations. Thanks to the unique format of this book, we can add to and expand it over time, based on your feedback. Please tell us what you think of the book, make suggestions for new content, and share your own experiences. You can send your feedback in three different ways:

1. Register your book and include your feedback in the comment section. You can register at http://www.passporter.com/register.asp.

2. Send an e-mail to ebooks@passporter.com.

3. Post on our message boards at http://www.passporterboards.com.

If you have tips, tricks, or magical memories about festivals and celebrations that you'd like to share, you may submit them through our Tips and Stories page at http://www.passporter.com/customs/tipsandstories.asp. This also enters you in our ongoing contest, and you could win a free copy of one of our books!

If you have photos of particular events to share, please upload them to the PassPorter Photo Archive at http://www.passporter.com/photos.

We look forward to hearing from you!

Jennifer and Dave Marx
Publishers

Beautiful butterfly spotted during the Flower & Garden Festival at Epcot

30% Discount Coupon

Save 30% off <u>any</u> PassPorter guidebook when you order direct from the publisher!

How to order a PassPorter at your 30% discount:
1. Visit http://www.passporterstore.com/store to view our guidebooks and place an order (type in this discount code during checkout: brits).
2. Call us toll-free at <u>877-WAYFARER</u> (that's 1-877-929-3273) and mention the "festivals" code when placing your order.

This offer valid only for direct book sales through PassPorter Travel Press, an imprint of MediaMarx, Inc. Offer not valid in bookstores. Cannot be combined with other discounts. Discount code: paris

Partial PassPorter Title List

All of the following titles are eligible for your 30% discount!

PassPorter's Walt Disney World—The unique travel guide, planner, organizer, journal, and keepsake! (spiral, deluxe starter kit, and refill kit)

PassPorter's Disney 500—A tried-and-true collection of more than 500 tips for Walt Disney World trips (paperback)

PassPorter's Disney Vacation Club—Tips for members and members-to-be, filled with practial information! (paperback)

PassPorter's Open Mouse for Walt Disney World—Easy-Access Trips for Travelers With Extra Challenges. Covers virtually every special challenge! (paperback)

PassPorter's Disney Cruise Line and Its Ports of Call—The take-along travel guide and planner. The most comprehensive guide to Disney cruising! (paperback)

PassPorter's Disney Cruise Clues—A tried-and-true collection of more than 250 tips for Disney Cruise Line vacations. (paperback)

PassPorter's Disneyland Resort and Southern California Attractions—The unique travel guide, planner, organizer, journal, and keepsake! (spiral, deluxe starter kit, and refill kit)

PassPorter's Treasure Hunts at Walt Disney World—Discover what everyone else is missing with more than 100+ hunts for a variety of ages and skills (paperback)

More information about PassPorter's innovative guidebooks and descriptions of each of the above titles are on the following pages.

PassPorter's Club

Do you want more help planning your Disney vacation? Join the PassPorter's Club and get all these benefits:

✔ "All-you-can-read" access to EVERY e-book we publish (12 titles at press time). PassPorter's Club passholders also get early access to these e-books before the general public. New e-books are added on a regular basis, too.

✔ Interactive, customizable "e-worksheets" to help make your trip planning easier, faster, and smoother. These are the electronic, interactive worksheets we've been mentioning throughout this book. The worksheets are in PDF format and can be printed for a truly personalized approach! We have more than 50 worksheets, with more on the way. You can see a sample e-worksheet to the right.

✔ Access to super-sized "e-photos" in the PassPorter Photo Archives—photos can be zoomed in up to 25 times larger than standard web photos. You can use these e-photos to see detail as if you're actually standing there—or use them for desktop wallpaper, scrapbooking, whatever!

✔ Our best discount on print guidebooks ... 35% off!

There's more features, too! For a full list of features and current e-books, e-worksheets, and e-photos, visit http://www.passporter.com/club. You can also take a peek inside the Club's Gallery at http://www.passporterboards.com/forums/passporters-club-gallery. The Gallery is open to everyone—it contains two FREE interactive e-worksheets to try out!

Price: A PassPorter's Club pass is currently $4.95/month, or the cost of just one e-book!

How to Get Your Pass to the PassPorter's Club

Step 1. Get a free community account. Register simply and quickly at http://www.passporterboards.com/forums/register.php.

Step 2. Log in at http://www.passporterboards.com/forums/login.php using the Member Name and password you created in step 1.

Step 3. Get your pass. Select the type of pass you'd like and follow the directions to activate it immediately. We currently offer monthly and annual passes. (Annual passes save 25% and get extra perks!)

Questions? Assistance? We're here to help! Please send e-mail to club@passporter.com.

You may also find many of your questions answered in our FAQ (Frequently Asked Questions) in the Gallery forum (see link above).

What Is PassPorter?

PassPorters are unique, all-in-one travel guides that offer comprehensive, expert advice and innovative planning systems. Many of our guidebooks feature built-in worksheets and organizer "PassPockets." The PassPockets help you organize your vacation by building trip itineraries on the front before you go, storing maps, passes, and receipts inside while you're there, recording memories and expenses on the back to enjoy when you return.

PassPorter Walt Disney World Resort

It all started with Walt Disney World (and a mouse)! Our general Walt Disney World guidebook covers everything you need to plan a practically perfect vacation, including fold-out park maps; full-color photos and charts; resort room layout diagrams; KidTips; descriptions, reviews, and ratings for the resorts, parks, attractions, and restaurants; and much more!

This edition also includes 14 organizer pockets you can use to plan your trip before you go, hold papers while you're there, and record your memories for when you return. The PassPockets are our readers' #1 favorite feature because they make planning, organizing, and capturing your vacation very easy.

Learn more and order at http://www.passporter.com, or get a copy at your favorite bookstore. Our Walt Disney World guide is available in a spiral-bound edition, and a Deluxe Edition in a ring binder with interior pockets is also available—see the next page.

Don't take our word for it—ask others what they think of PassPorter. Here's a letter we recently received (printed with permission).

Listen, I'm not well organized. OK, that's an understatement. I'm a mess. I don't plan either. I'm more fly by the seat of my pants. However, 6 years ago on my honeymoon, my husband and I wandered aimlessly around Disney World and didn't get to see half the stuff we wanted and didn't even know about the other half.

So, my first trip with my daughter would have to be different. I found the boards at http://www.disboards.com and asked what book I needed to buy. Most everyone suggested yours. "What would I do with pockets?" I asked myself.

Through the planning stages, I found myself furiously writing different phone numbers, confirmation numbers, and other important information into my Passporter. I stuffed all kinds of information and plans into those pockets.

When we got to Disney, my husband could not believe how organized I was. Check-ins were a breeze. I had all the information I needed at my fingertips. I think his mouth was hanging open at one point. He'd say, "What's on the agenda for today?" And I'd whip out my book and tell him.

I had touring plans so we knew exactly where to go when. The lady at the Rainforest Café could not believe I had all my info right there. I think she thought I am always that organized. (Can you make a Passporter for my regular life?)

My vacation could not have gone any smoother and I owe it all to you!

Thanks so much,
Sydonie Davis

More PassPorters

You've asked for more PassPorters—we've listened! We have four PassPorter print books and ten e-books (and growing), all designed to make your Disney vacation the best it can be. And if you've wished for a PassPorter with all the flexibility and features of a daily planner, check out our Deluxe Editions (described below). To learn more about the new PassPorters and get release dates, please visit us at http://www.passporter.com.

PassPorter's Walt Disney World Deluxe Edition

Design first-class vacations with this loose-leaf ring binder edition. The Deluxe Edition features the same great content as *PassPorter's Walt Disney World* spiral guide. Special features of the Deluxe Edition include ten interior storage slots in the binder to hold guidemaps, ID cards, and a pen (we even include a pen). The Deluxe PassPorter binder makes it really easy to add, remove, and rearrange pages ... you can even download, print, and add in updates, feature articles, and supplemental pages from our web site, and refills are available for purchase. Learn more at http://www.passporter.com/wdw/deluxe.htm. The Deluxe Edition is available through bookstores by special order—the ISBN is 978-1-58771-083-4 (2011 Deluxe Edition), or search for the latest edition.

PassPorter's Disney Cruise Line and its Ports of Call

Updated annually! Get your cruise plans in shipshape with our updated, award-winning field guide ... includes details on all new ports and the new ships to come! Authors Jennifer and Dave Marx cover the Disney Cruise Line in incredible detail, including deck plans, stateroom floor plans, original photos, menus, entertainment guides, port/shore excursion details, and plenty of worksheets to help you budget, plan, and record your information. We also include reader tips, photos, and magial memories! In its ninth edition in 2011, this is the original and most comprehensive guidebook devoted to the Disney Cruise Line! Learn more and order your copy at http://www.passporter.com/dcl or get a copy at your favorite bookstore. ISBN for the eighth edition paperback, no PassPockets is 978-1-58771-079-7. Also available in a Deluxe Edition with organizer PassPockets (ISBN: 978-1-58771-080-3).

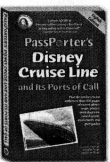

Even More PassPorters

PassPorter's Disneyland Resort and Southern California Attractions– Second Edition

PassPorter tours the park that started it all in this updated book! California's Disneyland, Disney's California Adventure, and Downtown Disney get PassPorter's expert treatment, and we throw in Hollywood and Downtown Los Angeles, San Diego, SeaWorld, the San Diego Zoo and Wild Animal Park, LEGOLAND, and Six Flags Magic Mountain. All this, and PassPorter's famous PassPockets and planning features.Our second edition follows the same format as the 2010 edition of PassPorter's Walt Disney World, complete with glossy, full-color pages, tons of photos from your authors and fellow readers, and plenty of brand-new pages! We een include the special photo supplement at the end to get you in the mood for our California vacation. Whether you're making the pilgrimage to Disneyland for a big celebration or planning a classic Southern California family vacation, you can't miss. Learn more at http://www.passporter.com/dl, or pick it up at your favorite bookstore (ISBN: 978-1-58771-042-1). This guidebook is also available as a Deluxe Edition in a padded, six-ring binder (ISBN: 978-1-58771-043-8).

PassPorter's Treasure Hunts at Walt Disney World

Have even more fun at Walt Disney World! Jennifer and Dave's treasure hunts have long been a favorite part of PassPorter reader gatherings at Walt Disney World, and now you can join in the fun. Gain a whole new appreciation of Disney's fabulous attention to detail as you search through the parks and resorts for the little (and big) things that you may never have noticed before. Great for individuals, families, and groups, with hunts for people of all ages and levels of Disney knowledge. Special, "secure" answer pages make sure nobody can cheat. Learn more, see sample hunts, and order your copy at http://www.passporter.com/hunts or get a copy at your favorite bookstore (ISBN: 978-1-58771-026-1).

PassPorter E-Books

We have many e-books that cover narrower topics in delightful depth! See all the details at http://www.passporterstore.com/store/ebooks.aspx. And watch for select e-books to make it into print in the near future.

PassPorter E-Books

Looking for more in-depth coverage on specific topics? Look no further than PassPorter E-Books! Our e-books are inexpensive (from $5.95–$8.95) and available immediately as a download on your computer (Adobe PDF format). If you prefer your books printed, we have options for that, too! And unlike most e-books, ours are fully formatted just like a regular PassPorter print book. A PassPorter e-book will even fit into a Deluxe PassPorter Binder, if you have one. We offer 12 e-books, at press time, and have plans for many, many more!

PassPorter's Disney 500: *Fast Tips for Walt Disney World Trips*
Our most popular e-book has more than 500 time-tested Walt Disney World tips—all categorized and coded! We chose the best of our reader-submitted tips over a six-year period for this e-book and each has been edited by author Jennifer Marx. For more details, a list of tips, and a sample page, visit http://www.passporter.com/wdw/disney500.asp.

PassPorter's Cruise Clues: *First-Class Tips for Disney Cruise Trips*
Get the best tips for the Disney Cruise Line—all categorized and coded—as well as cruise line comparisons, a teen perspective, and ultimate packing lists! This popular e-book is packed with 250 cruiser-tested tips—all edited by award-winning author Jennifer Marx. Visit http://www.passporter.com/dcl/cruiseclues.asp.

PassPorter's Disney Character Yearbook
A 268-page compendium of all the live Disney characters you can find at Walt Disney World, Disneyland, and on the Disney Cruise Line. Also includes tips on finding, meeting, photographing, and getting autographs, plus a customizable autograph book to print! Visit http://www.passporter.com/disney-character-yearbook.asp.

PassPorter's Disney Speed Planner: *The Easy Ten-Step Program*
A fast, easy method for planning practically perfect vacations—great for busy people or those who don't have lots of time to plan. Follow this simple, ten-step plan to help you get your vacation planned in short order so you can get on with your life. It's like a having an experienced friend show you the ropes—and have fun doing it! Visit http://www.passporter.com/wdw/speedplanner.asp.

PassPorter's Free-Book
A Guide to Free and Low-Cost Activities at Walt Disney World
It's hard to believe anything is free at Walt Disney World, but there are actually a number of things you can get or do for little to no cost. This e-book documents more than 150 free or cheap things to do before you go and after you arrive. Visit http://www.passporter.com/wdw/free-book.asp.

PassPorter's Sidekick for the Walt Disney World Guidebook
An interactive collection of worksheets, journal pages, and charts
This is a customizable companion to our general Walt Disney World guidebook—you can personalize worksheets, journals, luggage tags, and charts, plus click links to all the URLs in the guidebook and get transportation pages for all points within Walt Disney World! Details at http://www.passporter.com/wdw/sidekick.asp.

PassPorter's Festivals and Celebrations
at Walt Disney World
Get in on all the fun in this updated 78-page overview of all the wonderful and magical festivals, celebrations, parties, and holidays at Walt Disney World. Included are beautiful color photos and tips on maximizing your experience at the festivals and celebrations. Read more and see a sample page at http://www. passporter.com/wdw/festivals-celebrations.asp.

PassPorter's Answer Book
Get answers to the most popular topics asked about Walt Disney World, Disneyland, Disney Cruise Line, and general travel. You've asked it, we've answered it! The e-book's questions and answers are sorted geographically and topically. The e-book is authored by our amazing PassPorter Guide Team, who have heaps of experience at answering your questions! Details at http://www.passporter. com/answer-book.asp.

PassPorter's Disney Weddings & Honeymoons
This is both a guidebook and a bridal organizer tailored to the unique requirements of planning a wedding, vow renewal, or commitment ceremony at Walt Disney World or on the Disney Cruise Line. It will take you through the entire process, outline your options, offer valuable tips, organize your information, and help you plan your event down to the last detail! Details at http://www. passporter.com/weddings.asp.

PassPorter's Disney Vacation Club Guide
A 170-page in-depth guide to all aspects of the Disney Vacation Club, from deciding whether to join to deciding where and when to use your points. Included are beautiful color photos and tips on maximizing your experience. If you've ever wondered what the club is all about or wanted to learn more, this is the perfect introduction. Visit http://www.passporter.com/disney-vacation-club.asp.

Learn more about these and other titles and order e-books at:
http://www.passporterstore.com/store/ebooks.aspx

Register Your PassPorter

We are <u>very</u> interested to learn how your vacation went and what you think of the PassPorter, how it worked (or didn't work) for you, and your opinion on how we could improve it! We encourage you to register your copy of PassPorter with us—in return for your feedback, we'll send you **two valuable coupons** good for discounts on PassPorters and PassHolder pouches when purchased directly from us. You can register your copy of PassPorter at http://www.passporterboards.com/forums/club/books.php, or you can send us a postcard or letter to P.O. Box 3880, Ann Arbor, Michigan 48106.

Report a Correction or Change

Keeping up with the changes at Walt Disney World is virtually impossible without your help. When you notice something is different than what is printed in PassPorter, or you just come across something you'd like to see us cover, please let us know! You can report your news, updates, changes, corrections, and even rumors (everything helps!) at http://www.passporter.com/report.asp.

Contribute to the Next Edition

You can become an important part of future editions of PassPorter! The easiest way is to rate the resorts, rides, and/or eateries at http://www.passporter.com/wdw/rate.htm. Your ratings and comments become part of our reader ratings throughout the book and help future readers make travel decisions. Want to get more involved? Send us a vacation tip or magical memory—if we use it in a future edition of PassPorter, we'll credit you by name in the guidebook and send you a free copy of the edition!

Get Your Questions Answered

We love to hear from you! Alas, due to the thousands of e-mails and hundreds of phone calls we receive each week we cannot offer personalized advice to all our readers. But there's a great way to get your questions answered: ask your fellow readers! Visit our message boards at http://www.passporterboards.com, join for free, and post your question. In most cases, fellow readers and Disney fans will offer their ideas and experiences! Our message boards also function as an ultimate list of frequently asked questions. Just browsing through to see the answers to other readers questions will reap untold benefit! This is also a great way to make friends and have fun while planning your vacation. But be careful—our message boards can be addictive!

PassPorter Online

A wonderful way to get the most from your PassPorter is to visit our active web site at http://www.passporter.com. We serve up valuable PassPorter updates, plus useful Walt Disney World information and advice we couldn't jam into our book. You can swap tales (that's t-a-l-e-s, Mickey!) with fellow Disney fans, play contests and games, find links to other sites, get plenty of details, and ask us questions. You can also order PassPorters and shop for PassPorter accessories and travel gear! The latest information on new PassPorters to other destinations is available on our web site as well.

PassPorter Web Sites	Address (URL)
Main Page: PassPorter Online	http://www.passporter.com
Walt Disney World Forum	http://www.passporter.com/wdw
PassPorter Posts Message Boards	http://www.passporterboards.com
Book Updates	http://www.passporter.com/customs/bookupdates.htm
Rate the Rides, Resorts, Restaurants	http://www.passporter.com/wdw/rate.htm
Register Your PassPorter	http://www.passporter.com/register.asp
PassPorter Deluxe Edition Information	http://www.passporter.com/wdw/deluxe.htm